PRACTICE LESS, PLAY MORE!

The simple, three-step system to play
songs you love on your guitar from day 1

Steve Mastroianni (aka VØID)

ISBN-13: 978-1-7951621-5-9

This book was created for everyone who has great music in them, but doesn't know how to get it out.

That was me 22 years ago, so I would like to dedicate this book to my late father Tony, who had to endure the worst of my practice sessions and always remained my biggest fan.

I love you Dad.

Tony Mastroianni (aka Papa VØID)
September 2nd, 1954 - April 27th, 2015

DOWNLOAD THE AUDIOBOOK FREE!

READ THIS FIRST

Just to say thanks for buying my book,
I would like to give you the Audiobook version of
PRACTICE LESS, PLAY MORE! 100% FREE!

TO DOWNLOAD GO TO:

PracticeLessPlayMore.com/audiobook

WHAT OTHERS ARE SAYING ABOUT STEVE (AKA VØID)

"VØID, you are one special guy."

GENE SIMMONS - Co-Founder of KISS

"Steve's ability to connect with his audience, understand their needs, and quickly solve their most frustrating problems in the simplest way possible is second to none. Steve is an incredible Guitar Player, talented coach, and an amazing human being."

CHARLIE WALLACE -
Founder of Guitar Mastery Method

"What I like about Steve's approach is he finds the solution for your situation.

I have problems with my hands…Steve finds a way for me to play the songs without the pain I usually have. With my memory issues, Steve has come up with ideas that have helped with my memory I would have never thought of."

Steve, you have helped me more in the last couple years than all the private lessons I've taken!!

GREG R. - Beginner Guitarist from Mentor, Ohio

"If you wanna take the stress and struggle out of learning guitar, then Steve's your man."

JON H. - Beginner Guitarist from Abercarn, Wales

"If you really want to play guitar, Steve will show you the quickest way possible.

Not just chords and notes, but A LOT MORE. Like: What, When, Where, Why and How.

All while actually playing the guitar along with your favorite records."

DOUG F. - Beginner Guitarist from Aurora, USA

"Steve's coaching helps me play & sing my favorite songs almost immediately.

I tell Steve the song I want to learn and he sends me the simplified instructions so I can play right away.

I played "Wonderful Tonight" for my wife on our 29th Anniversary and she was amazed!!

Says she listens to the recording when she needs cheering up.

Happy wife, happy life!

And now I'm even planning my first Open Mic! I can't believe it's only been 90 days since I started playing!"

PHILIP C. - Beginner Guitarist from USA

"Steve breaks everything down to its simplest form and then shows you how to build it up again from playing chords to playing along in perfect time with the record.

My partner used to cringe when I practiced...now she's making song requests. It's great!"

TONY C. - Beginner Guitarist from Wales

CONTENTS

FOREWORD

MAKING MUSIC OUT OF CHAOS

I know a thing or two about challenges.

Whether it was…

- being pressured by my record label to write a hit song while touring the world opening for bands like KISS, Hinder, and Finger Eleven (during a time when ZERO Rock bands were on the charts)…
- becoming my father's primary caregiver after he was diagnosed with stage IV colon cancer and inspiring him to find the strength to get back on the golf course in his final months…

OR

- providing for my family by running two music-based businesses from home while helping my wife take care of our baby daughter in her first year of life…

I've had many puzzles to solve in my life so far.

And the only thing that kept me strong through the toughest times was my love of making music.

At any point, the easiest thing to do would have been to quit playing altogether.

However, I think what makes life most interesting is learning how to weather the storm and come out the other side successfully.

That's what this book is all about.

If you're like me and you always have a calendar full of commitments, yet you have an obsession with playing guitar…

Then I'm so happy we met because this book will help you play the best music of your life.

It will help you weather any storm YOU currently have in your life and give you the tools you need to help you win the game of playing guitar.

LET YOURSELF BE OBSESSED

If you have a guitar, 5-10 minutes of free time per day, and the desire to play…

You have everything you need to play the songs you love.

If …

- You tried to play guitar in the past and failed…
- You are making excuses right now why you can't do it or it won't work for you…

OR

- You can't find the time in your super busy schedule…

It's ok.

You just didn't have a method that gives you results you're happy with.

Once you get the results, you get inspired...

You get obsessed...

You get your credit card out at 2 o'clock in the morning to purchase things you don't need for your guitar.

And most importantly, you make the time to play more guitar.

We make time for things that make us happy and get us results.

No one understands this better than I do.

I've been wanting to write this book for years.

I also had every excuse NOT to write this book...

"I'm too busy."

"It's too much work."

"I'll start writing the book next year when I have more time."

All it took was a random string of events on a random Friday to inspire me to take action and finally start writing.

Don't question it.

Ride that wave of inspiration when you get it.

Be obsessed with it and let it guide you to where you need to go.

Whether it's learning "Dark Side Of The Moon" from front to back...

Or watching "The Song Remains The Same" 50 times because you're obsessed with matching Jimmy Page's guitar tone.

Just go with it.

It's good for you.

And when you AREN'T feeling inspired…

That's when books like this come in handy…

To give you a simple way to play songs you love on your guitar, day after day, no matter how much spare time you have.

And to lead you in a direction that gets you inspired again.

I was thinking of you the entire time I wrote this book and it makes me so happy that you have it in your hands right now because it contains lessons I've learned and mistakes I've made over the past 22 years SO YOU DON'T HAVE TO.

This book is your unfair advantage to playing your favourite songs on your guitar.

And I'm very proud to have written the whole thing in only 5 days in the most unlikely of conditions…

At home with an 11-month-old baby, a wife on maternity leave, and during Christmas craziness.

This book was MY obsession for 5 days straight and I rode the wave to completion to show you how when you have the right mindset, the right method, and the right coach, you can create incredible results in anything you set out to do.

As cliché as it sounds, if I can do it, then I promise you can too.

Remember, the conditions will never be perfect. Stop waiting.

Go make some music!

Rock on and talk soon,

Steve (aka VØID)

PREFACE

INTRODUCTION

"Yeah, but Jimi Hendrix wasn't cool!"

The sound of Gene Simmons' stoic voice still rings in my mind to this day.

It all started back in 2010 when my band The Envy was opening for KISS all over North America…

Freshly off of being signed by Gene on his new record label imprint Simmons Records.

The ink was still drying on the record contract.

The entire tour, Gene and I had our fair share of funny memories and debates…

Like the time in Jones Beach when Gene introduced me to his daughter Sophie for the first time…

…and then smacked me with a rolled-up magazine because he thought I was hitting on her.

All I said to her was, "Nice to meet you."!!!

Even 4 years later when I saw him backstage at the KISS show in Toronto, the first thing he said to me was (and I quote):

"VØID, you better behave yourself!"

The man NEVER forgets!

But I have to say, my absolute FAVOURITE memory of the tour was what Gene said to me when I was on stage at soundcheck in Atlanta...

Hours before playing Aaron's Amphitheatre in front of THOUSANDS of screaming fans.

Before I tell you about what he said to me at soundcheck...

Let me tell you about what led up to that day, so you get the most from this story...

BACKSTAGE BACKSTORY

It was right after The Envy played our first show in Pittsburgh, when Gene crashed our dressing room, rainbow cake in hand, and pulled me aside.

Good thing I still had my clothes on.

You have to understand that I had known Gene for about a year at this point, so "surprises" like this were to be expected.

But I have to say, NOTHING would prepare me for what he was about to say next.

Which would begin a three-week chapter of the KISS tour that I would never forget...

So there I was in my dressing room...

Sweat still dripping from my face from the 45-minute concert I just finished playing.

Between the radio performance I did in the morning and that night's concert at First Niagara Pavilion (now the KeyBank Pavilion) in Pittsburgh, PA.

(the first show of a 34 date North American support slot for KISS)...

This was a LONG day.

And the last thing I could process was the advice I was about to get from a guy who was LITERALLY wearing 9-inch platforms in front of me! ;)

I said, "Gene, what are you doing here? Don't you have to get ready for the show?"

And he said, "Yes VØID, but first I have to talk to you about something important."

MY DEMON MENTOR

One thing you should know about Gene...

Is that he LOVES giving advice!

(I guess the two of us share that in common)

So when Gene speaks, I listen.

"What is it Gene?"...I played along.

Even though at that point...

All I wanted to do was head to the merch booth to hang out with fans, take pictures, and sign autographs.

But that's when Gene put his mentor cap on and said,

"You know, VØID, you did a great job out there. I want you to know that."

I was shocked by what he said…

And just as I was about to say thanks…

"Hey, thanks Ge…"

Is when Gene continued…

"But I REALLY think you would look cooler if you lowered your guitar like this…"

And he proceeded to get into Rock God mode and actually SHOW me how he wanted me to stand on stage.

Oh man…I couldn't believe what was happening before my eyes…

Being on the KISS Tour in the first place was pretty damn surreal…

But Gene Simmons actually squatting in full costume to give me guitar posing advice was on a WHOLE new level!

Honestly though, that was NOTHING compared to what happened next.

A DEMON-STRATION I'LL NEVER FORGET

I was never really a true KISS fan.

Sure, I could recognize a KISS tune here and there, but KISS was never really a band I listened to growing up.

I did grow to have a list of favourite songs after hearing the KISS Army chanting them night after night for 3 months.

I was actually more of a fan of Gene - the man, the myth, the legend.

And I knew Gene Simmons to do MANY things:

- Create business empires
- Have a lifetime of wisdom to share
- and perform at a world class level even at 60+ years old

However, I would have NEVER imagined

That he would hound me for 3 weeks on tour

To do something as specific as lowering my guitar.

And I mean EVERY DAY…

EVERY chance he got!

When Gene has his mind on something, he doesn't let up.

He even recruited KISS drummer Eric Singer to get in on the action.

Together they would actually act out how they wanted me to pose on stage.

(I guess you can't spell "demonstrate" without DEMON, right?)

It felt like the Rock version of *The Karate Kid* every day at catering!

What's a guy gotta do to eat his peach cobbler in peace without getting harassed by Rock legends???

I'm still figuring out the answer to that question.

That was NOTHING compared to what happened next...

FAMOUS LAST WORDS

Before each show, my band The Envy would have 45 minutes of uninterrupted time to sound check everything and make sure all of our equipment was working properly and sounding great.

But today was different...and I could feel it.

It was August 31st, 2010 and we were at Aaron's Amphitheatre in Atlanta, GA about to play in front of a screaming crowd of over 10,000 people.

It was going to be awesome!

I noticed Gene in the corner of my eye, side stage, chatting with some investors for an upcoming business investment he was planning.

(This guy never stops!)

So you could imagine my surprise...

When he excused himself for a second so he could come to chat with ME...

I think you know what's coming.

"Hey VØID, I see you've lowered your guitar."

I did...and was glad he noticed.

I thought I was finally off the hook.

3 weeks of daily chirping would finally come to an end and we could discuss other things like maybe…ummmmm…the future of my band??? ;)

Nope.

Not today.

Not until Gene got what he wanted.

"I still think your guitar could be lower."

Can you believe this guy?

By the way…

My guitar height wasn't an accident.

I set it as a happy balance that was high enough for optimal playing…

…and low enough not to look like a total dork.

So I fired back with this: "You know, Gene, Fender Strats need to be played a little higher because of the length of the fretboard."

Which is absolutely true.

If you wear a Fender Strat too low, then you'll have a tough time reaching the thinner strings and higher frets.

At least I do.

Gene fires back with this gem.

He said, "VØID, there isn't ONE cool guitarist who plays his Strat that high."

(It wasn't even that high…it was at my belt buckle!)

So I said, "Of course there are. Like Jimi Hendrix."

I had a smirk on my face that you could see all the way from the box office.

I finally got him!

Even my singer and the KISS crew stopped what they were doing and were listening in on our exchange.

I bested the best chirper I've ever met…

…or at least I thought I did.

Jimi Hendrix is highly regarded as one of the greatest guitarists in history…

Most people would agree he was a true pioneer and one of the most influential guitarists who ever existed.

Jimi played a Fender Strat and if you look at old performance photos, he wore it at pretty much the same height as I was wearing it (if not higher).

And I think he had a pretty decent career. ;)

I mean, as far as I know his guitar strap height had nothing to do with his massive success and it definitely didn't prevent him from becoming immortalized as a guitar god, right?

But logic doesn't always win an argument…

Not on that fine August afternoon.

Not when you're discussing strap height with Gene Simmons.

Gene pauses for a moment to collect his thoughts…

Looks at me…

And says…

"But Jimi Hendrix wasn't cool."

And then he walks away…

Back to his investors…

Resuming his meeting…

Without skipping a beat!

My jaw hit the floor.

I couldn't believe what just happened.

Our soundcheck was a write-off because I was laughing so hard.

How funny is this guy?

Gene is one of my favourite people because despite his on-stage theatrics and off-stage stoicism…

He's just a loveable geek living the Rockstar life.

And he'll do anything to get the last laugh.

I mean, how can you argue with that kind of stubbornness and confidence?

Well, that was the LAST straw!

BEGINNING AGAIN

I couldn't take it anymore, so I finally gave in!

I set my strap to the lowest possible setting for our show later that night in Atlanta.

And I had to relearn the set with a ridiculously low guitar…

All to please (and hopefully quiet) the demon of Rock.

I drastically changed my guitar setup hours before playing a show to a crowd of over 10,000 people in Atlanta.

And all because of Gene's simple request.

But I'm a team player, so I wanted to play ball.

What's one night going to affect, right?

So there I was, re-learning my entire setlist…

…a setlist containing original songs that I wrote and played hundreds of times…

…and I was struggling to play MY OWN guitar parts.

The Riffs, the solos…

EVERYTHING!

And since I was the main guitarist in the band…

I was the one responsible for holding down the majority of the Rhythm section, which included Open Chords, Barre Chords, and some complex shapes that were tricky to play even with my regular strap setting.

I've lowered my guitar a bit in the past...

But this was SO much lower than I've ever played and it felt like I was learning to play guitar for the first time.

I couldn't pull off a basic move like play a SINGLE Barre Chord or even play some of the easiest lead parts in the set...

...without feeling like my hand was about to break off!

And I've been playing guitar for 15 years at this point!

THE RESULT?

So what happened at the show later that night?

Did I look like a total Rockstar?

Cooler than Hendrix playing his fiery guitar at Monterey?

Realizing Gene's vision of pure, low-strap, Rock God-ery?

Well...

Not quite.

I'm going to go on record right here and tell you...

There's absolutely NO WAY all those mistakes I made in Atlanta made me look cool!

It was brutal.

Constant adjustments to my guitar...

Botched chords…

Missed strings…

It was my worst show of the tour from a playing perspective…

By the third song, I asked my guitar tech to put the strap setting back to normal.

So I could redeem myself by putting on a good show and save my left hand from falling off!

And luckily, I did.

From then on, my strap setting has <u>NEVER</u> changed.

LESSONS LEARNED

I shared this story with you to teach you two VERY important lessons:

1) The ingredients REALLY matter.

Your guitar setup, how you practice, and your overall approach to guitar playing will be the difference between struggling to play for years and the best guitar playing of your life.

This book will help you with the latter by giving you simple strategies you can use right away to cut your learning time in half and increase your confidence.

It will shed light on the elements that threaten your success on guitar and make you aware of how everything "fits" together, so you can make the fastest progress possible.

With that said…

2) ALWAYS take the guitar advice you receive with a grain of salt.

Even the advice in this book.

Especially when it comes from a 7-foot-tall demon with an army behind him!

There's actually WAY more to this story beyond what I wrote here

(especially what happened right after Gene played the last note of "Rock and Roll All Nite" and walked backstage)

But we'll have to save that one for another day…and probably for a video, so I can actually show you what Gene did. ;)

When it comes to opinions about how you should play guitar, you gotta do what works best for YOU!

No matter how against the grain it is to traditions and popular beliefs.

If you are currently getting results you're happy with, then you have to keep doing what's working for you.

And if you aren't getting results (which might be why you're reading this book right now), then you need to find an approach that works for you ASAP.

Just know there is NO such thing as a one-size-fits-all solution for your guitar playing.

ANYWHERE!

This book contains a simple system you can use to learn the songs you love on guitar in the least amount of time possible and is the closest thing to a one-size-fits-all solution that I've ever come across.

Feel free to modify the system only AFTER you've experienced it for yourself.

Just keep an open mind and give it a shot…

…like I did with my guitar strap that night in Atlanta.

I promise you'll have a better time than I did. ;)

Why Write a Book About Practicing?

Good question!

Put simply: This book is long overdue.

In a world where there are millions of guitar videos to sift through online and barely any time to watch them…

A world with distraction and overwhelm around every corner…

A world filled with too many empty promises and too little results…

Something had to be done.

And fast!

Because too many Beginner Guitarists are giving up on their dream too soon…

Too many are struggling to play the same songs for weeks and not knowing what to do about it…

Dusty guitars are becoming an epidemic.

After 22 years of being a self-taught player, 10 years of playing professionally, and 16 years of teaching adults how to play their favourite songs on guitar, I've learned A LOT about what works and what doesn't.

I find it to be such a tragedy when I hear about Beginners & Struggling Guitarists who have the greatest of intentions to play guitar, but get completely derailed because they have of a lack of direction and a lack of expert guidance.

It doesn't have to be so hard!

With the right information & insights, more people who have the desire to play would be making beautiful music on their guitars right now.

You have A LOT of great music inside of you.

You just don't know how to get it all out.

I always knew that if I could get my time-saving strategies into your hands and walk you through my simple system of learning new songs on guitar, I could help inspire you and guide you to the Promised Land.

And that's how "PRACTICE LESS, PLAY MORE!" was born.

The PRACTICE LESS, PLAY MORE! system is VERY easy to learn…

And like any great system, it…

Saves
You
Stress
Time
Energy and
Money

Your time is way too valuable and your dream of playing guitar is way too important to waste on guessing what to do next and going down the rabbit hole of online lessons without getting any meaningful results.

There IS an easier way to play guitar and you CAN learn to play guitar in less time when you learn from someone who has already made all the mistakes so you don't have to.

So my aim for this book is to get you your time back, get the guitar in your hands, and help you achieve your dream of playing your favourite songs in the least amount of time possible.

Because I know firsthand how great it feels to play guitar effortlessly and I want you to experience it for yourself.

DISCLAIMER

I get a lot of flak online when I use words like "shortcut", "easy way to play guitar", or basically promise any kind of result that doesn't involve practicing in a gruelling, mind-numbing way.

(You can check out my Facebook page or YouTube channel in the links section if you want to hear more about the hate mail I receive and my reaction to it)

So before we get started, I have to say the following:

This book will NOT make you Hendrix in a day, Clapton in a week, or SRV in a month.

You will NOT be able to magically play your favourite songs if all you do is read this book.

You have to do the work to get the results.

Fortunately, I've made the process as easy as possible for you.

So you can do less work in less time.

And get consistent, noticeable results you can be happy with.

* * * *

This book does NOT contain every possible song you can ever learn.

In fact, it doesn't have ANY song tutorials in it at all.

You may be surprised to find there are NO scales, NO exercises, and NO chord diagrams to learn in this book.

That's because you can find all of that stuff online.

(I'll show you how to find it and exactly what to do with it when you do)

What this book WILL do is equip you with a simple three-step system that will give you both clarity & confidence...

...as well as enable you to learn the songs you set out to play on guitar in way less time than any conventional approach you may have tried.

As you can probably tell by the title of the book, "PRACTICE LESS, PLAY MORE!" is focused on learning the guitar by PLAYING SONGS, and it will show you how to do it in a way that is easy to follow...

Saving you time, energy, and a ton of frustration...

So you can experience the joy & confidence that comes from playing the songs you love on your own terms.

WHO IS THIS BOOK FOR?

This book is ideal for you if:

1) You're a Beginner Guitarist who just started learning to play guitar.

You're excited, intimidated, and a bit overwhelmed about playing guitar and where it fits into your life.

This book will give you the tools & techniques you can use to easily get guitar into your schedule and start playing along with your favourite songs right away.

2) You've been playing guitar for longer than a year and you're stuck in a rut.

Playing guitar has become VERY challenging for you and you can't really play anything you're happy with. You're working through the same old stuff every time you pick up the guitar, and you just can't make any progress, so you pick it up less & less often. You're feeling uninspired and you aren't sure what you're doing wrong.

This book will help you regain your confidence and help you make steady progress, so you can finally get out of the rut and start playing the songs you've always wanted to play.

3) You're a Singer and/or Songwriter who wants to learn how to play guitar in the fastest way possible, so you can perform songs live and in the studio.

This book will give you the most efficient way to develop your guitar skills, so you can always keep your focus on the thing that matters most: your music.

* * * *

While this book is ideal for the 3 groups I listed above, it can also be used by guitarists of all levels - even with the busiest of schedules - because it is based on the way the brain learns and stores new information.

And since it is based on PLAYING SONGS, you will want to pick up the guitar more and more as you go…

…even if, right now, you can't imagine how you'll fit the guitar into your schedule.

The PRACTICE LESS, PLAY MORE! system is very easy to follow and I've done all the heavy lifting for you, so all you have to do is follow along, complete the actions, and enjoy the results!

* * * *

How Carnegie Hall Ruined The Guitar For Everyone

A pedestrian on 57th Street sees a musician getting out of a cab and asks, "How do you get to Carnegie Hall?"

Without pause, the artist replies wearily, "Practice Practice Practice".

* * * *

Oh man!

I can't tell you how many times I hear this joke and how a small part of me dies inside every time someone suggests Practice Practice Practice as a legitimate practice strategy.

Of course you need to practice…

Everyone knows that.

The guitar isn't going to magically play itself…

However, when you don't know how to play something on the guitar and someone with more experience than you tells you to simply *"Practice Practice Practice"*…

It can be incredibly frustrating.

I mean, how do you know WHAT to practice specifically?

And how do you know exactly HOW MANY TIMES to practice it so that you nail it quickly and don't spend more time on it than you need to?

It pains me whenever I see someone comment on my Facebook page when they've been trying to play something for weeks and instead of asking me for help, they automatically resort to "oh well, I guess I just need to Practice Practice Practice"…

Really? How has that approach been working for you so far?

Isn't it what got you in this mess in the first place?

I apologize for the mini rant, however I can't believe how quickly guitarists have adopted this empty saying as the unofficial slogan for guitar.

It seems like they never stop to think about how much time they are wasting by sitting down with their guitar and running in circles…

…still struggling with the same old stuff…

Sitting there practicing the same A minor pentatonic scale as you did for the past 6 months…

Wondering if it will ever sound like actual music.

At this rate, your guitar skills are NOT going to improve fast enough for you to stay motivated if your only strategy is sitting down with your guitar and repeating the same thing over and over again…

You might think you're making progress and maybe you are making a little bit here and there…

But it isn't predictable and it isn't really fun.

Without a clear strategy in place, your valuable time is being wasted without any guarantee of a result.

So if you've been relying on the 3 P's (Practice Practice Practice) as your main practice strategy and you're ready to upgrade to a much better, step-by-step strategy that guides you all the way from start to finish, then you're in for one hell of a ride!

Here are 3 major reasons why the Practice Practice Practice approach doesn't work:

- **It's too slow** - you might try to play the guitar part, make a mistake, start from the beginning, try again, make another mistake, start from the beginning, continuing like this for days, weeks, months, or years and you still aren't even guaranteed to get it.

  Sure, it's possible you might eventually get it, but it just takes too long and your guitar might be smashed to pieces before you do!

- **It isn't ideal for your brain** - when you burn yourself out over a guitar part through mindless repetition, eventually, your mind checks out and at that point, it isn't going to remember anything you're doing.

  And if your mind isn't remembering the part, your muscles definitely aren't.

  Rote memorization is not an efficient way to learn and you always run the risk of forgetting after a few months anyway.

- **It's too frustrating** - even if you are eventually able to play the riff, it probably came with so much frustration and stress that you don't even really like the song as much anymore.

So instead, of Practice Practice Practice…

The 3 P's you will learn in this book are PRIME, PRACTICE, and PLAY.

- **PRIME** will prepare you with my best mindsets & techniques for learning songs quickly, creating a no-fail practice habit, and getting the most out of your practice sessions…

- **PRACTICE** will lay out the same methodology that my students and I are using to learn new songs in a fraction of the time of conventional practice methods…

AND

- **PLAY** will give you my best mindsets & techniques to use when you are actually playing songs, so you can play as effortlessly as possible and have a blast doing it.

Each of the 3 P's gets its own section of the book, complete with explanations, practical examples, and actions you can take immediately to play more songs.

MY PROMISE TO YOU

I could tell you in great detail how I've helped my Beginner Guitar students like Doug F. or Enrique R. play dozens of their favourite songs within weeks, or how I've helped them create moments & memories with their significant other:

- like Steve F. did when he played his wife her favourite song on her 50th birthday
- Phil C. did when he played "Wonderful Tonight" for his wife on their 29th wedding anniversary

AND

- Jon H. did when he played "Chasing Cars" for his bride at their wedding

I could tell you all about how I've helped Ben D. and Pete G. cross "performing live" off their respective Bucket Lists while in their 60's.

I could even tell you how I've helped inspire guitarists like Dan. W, Chas D., and Johnny W. start writing & recording their own original songs when they could barely play a song on guitar before we met.

And sure, I could give you motivational one-liners like "If you believe it, you can achieve it" or make you some HUGE promises based on what I've helped other people achieve.

But I don't want this book to be filled with aspirational fluff that gets you thinking, 'One day I'll be able to ...'.

I want you to have a practical manual that you can use EVERY DAY to play songs you love on your guitar...

...so you can confidently say out loud "I'm a Guitar Player!"

* * * *

In this book, you will learn how to...

- Simplify the songs you're learning, so you can start playing them right away...
- Create a no-fail practice habit that works WITH your schedule rather than against it...
- Prepare the best materials for your practice sessions, so you don't waste ANY time while you have your guitar in hand...
- Practice in a simple, structured way that guarantees rapid results...

AND

- Learn what you should and shouldn't be thinking about while you're in Playing Mode.

I designed the book in a way that makes it very easy to take action at the end of every chapter.

With that in mind, I want to give you two quick examples of just how easy it is to increase your playing time and get musical results.

ONE: You might find yourself taking up a lot of your practice time watching video after video on YouTube, looking for that one simple tutorial video that will actually make sense and help you quickly play a song you love.

(Either that or you're watching videos of how kids react to "Mary Jane's Last Dance" when they hear it for the first time)

Only it's been 40 minutes and you've barely touched your guitar.

Instead of just being a passive observer, be an active player!

As the song is playing in the videos you're watching, focus on the drums and play along with the song by muting the guitar strings with your fretting hand (touching the strings lightly) and strumming along with Downstrokes to match the steady pulse of the music -

"1 2 3 4, 1 2 3 4, etc."

If you don't have your guitar with you, then you can tap the pulse on your desk or on your lap.

At least now you're playing music and working on your musical timing.

If the song is too fast, then you can use YouTube's speed function to drop the speed to 75% or 50% of the original speed and make it easier to play along with.

Result: Not only has your playing time increased, you'll also feel good that your musical timing is improving.

TWO: This tip is similar to the previous one. You might find that all of your practice time is being taken up by non-musical things like scales, exercises, and random chords switches - hoping that one day they will lead you to playing songs you love.

Stop right now.

(Especially if you can't play any songs yet)

Load up your favourite song right now, learn the first note or chord of the song and play Target Practice - where you pick or strum the first note or chord and play it every time it comes back around in the record *(usually every 4 bars)*.

For example, if your favourite song is "Back In Black", the first chord is E5, so every time the riff comes back around to E5 to start the sequence, play one E5 chord with a Downstroke to lock in with the record.

Result: This is way more fun to play and way more musical than practicing mind-numbing scales & exercises and having an empty Song Playlist. It also gives you something tangible to build on when you work on the rest of the song.

Do these two things sound too easy?

Good.

Because there's plenty more where that came from!

Let's head over to Chapter 1...

It's time to Practice Less, and PLAY More!

PART 1: PRIME

Chapter 1:
The Guitar Is Meant To
Play MUSIC!

Nobody ever dreamed of picking up a guitar and becoming a Guitar Practicer.

When we are wrapped up in that moment of pure inspiration…

- Attending an epic concert…
- Listening to a brand-new record from our favourite band…

OR

- Having our mind blown by a friend who rocked the "Sultans Of Swing" solo on their guitar right in front of our eyes…

We dream of becoming a Guitar PLAYER.

And Guitar Players play music.

Sure, we know practice will be involved in us getting there.

But we don't care because all we want to do is play music!

That's why I find it so interesting how backwards and unmusical a lot of guitar training is for Beginners.

Instead of focusing on PLAYING the same songs that inspired us to pick up a guitar in the first place, most of the attention in the first months is focused on prep work items like scales, exercises, and random chord shapes that are incredibly boring and unmusical.

And Adult Beginners blindly buy into "the process" because they assume that in order to become a great (or even decent) Guitar Player, they need to pay their dues by locking themselves away in a shed and practicing scales, exercises, and random chord shapes for at least 45-60 minutes per night.

Until their fingers bleed.

No pain, no gain, right?

Wrong!

This toxic thought is seriously robbing Beginners of the joy of playing music and instead is creating a culture of Beginners who blindly follow the destructive *"Practice Practice Practice"* motto I mentioned earlier.

Well, I can't just stand around and watch ambitious guitarists quitting on their dreams and making their guitars collect dust.

Not when I know I can help.

So that's why, for the past 16 years, I've made it part of my life's work to give Beginner Guitarists a better way to practice that is both fun and productive.

That way they can PLAY the songs they love as soon as possible.

Because I know what an influential role guitar has played in my own life and I want other guitarists to experience that same magic in theirs.

Remember, the guitar is a musical instrument, and it's meant to play MUSIC.

So a small part of me dies inside whenever I hear a Beginner Guitarist tell me about the scales they're working on when I full well know they can't even play a simple tune on the guitar.

What a tragedy.

Poor guy doesn't even know why he's practicing scales.

He just heard it was something you "should" know how to do.

Unfortunately, if he doesn't start playing songs soon…

He'll likely suffer the same fate as all the others who gave up on the guitar too early because they thought there was something wrong with them.

A little dramatic, I know, but over the past 16 years, I've talked to hundreds of Beginner Guitarists per week and I know they're on the fast track to a really bad situation with this traditional mentality unless we get them playing songs ASAP.

FIRST LESSON WITH A NEW STUDENT

When I start working with a new student, we usually talk about the bands/artists they love as well as the obstacles they're facing at the moment.

It often goes something like this when they reach out to me for help:

Them: *"Steve, I don't understand how I can practice every day and not make any progress on my guitar. How do I get out of this rut I'm stuck in?"*

Me: *"What do you practice when you sit down with the guitar?"*

And they usually tell me, *"I go through my chords and a few scales I learned from YouTube."*

Me: *"Anything else?"*

Them: *"Nope, that's pretty much it. I just sit down and play chords and scales for about 30 minutes and then I put the guitar down."*

Me: *"Ok, what songs can you play?"*

That's when I get the blank stare. ;)

Them: *"I can't play any songs yet."*

Me: *"Have you ever tried?"*

Them: *"Not really."*

Ummmm…what??? How is that possible?

They continue.

"I tried to put a few chords together, but my fingers take forever to switch between them."

Me: *"Ok, we have some work to do."*

And that's basically the extent of the conversation.

Can you believe some guys have been practicing like this for years?

Either getting stuck in a rut or playing on & off again for up to 30 years…

And not having ANY songs to show for it.

Sometimes not even making a single attempt!

Not on my watch.

I have to fix this!

When I dig deeper, I usually figure out why these guys aren't making any progress.

Often, it's because they don't have any structure or direction.

And if they've ever taken 1-on-1 lessons or joined an online training program, they clearly didn't get what they paid for because nothing changed.

They tend to think that by just picking up the guitar and playing ANYTHING for 30-60 minutes, they are going to get the results they want.

Luckily, I can save THESE guys because they reached out to me for help and they're in my Rockstar Mind ecosystem, so I can easily help them get the result they want.

I can't help but feel empathetic for the aspiring guitarists who don't reach out to me and are suffering in silence.

These guitarists are often completely in the dark about how to go about playing great tunes on their guitar.

GUITAR WARS: A NEW HOPE

Are you in the same situation right now?

If you are, it's ok.

If you've never learned how to practice in a way that quickly leads you to playing songs you love, then it isn't your fault.

You just never learned a better way and I don't blame you.

I mean, it's not like learning a proven practice strategy is the first thing you're dying to learn when you pick up a guitar for the first time.

But in my opinion, having an effective practice strategy you can rely on is the main difference between you successfully playing songs on your guitar and you struggling to play anything that sounds like real music for weeks, months, or even years.

My promise to you is that this system I'm about to share with you will be simple, fun, and will be based on you making great sounding music each step of the way.

Because if you have the pure desire to play guitar…

Then you deserve to play guitar WITHOUT having to spend all of your time HOPING that what you're practicing is actually going to lead you to the music you want to make.

In Chapter 7, you're going to learn a new approach to practicing called a Fast Practice Session, which will be the key to helping you practice less, and play more.

Before we dive into what a Fast Practice Session looks like and how to use it to make music, let's first take a look at what an inefficient practice session looks like…

And how it is the farthest thing from you making recognizable music on guitar.

Think about your own practice sessions while you read the list and tell me if any (or all) of these sound familiar:

Do you…

…start learning a new song by trying to play the exact guitar parts on the record at full speed?

…practice the same guitar part over & over again from the beginning until you get tired or bored?

…pick up the guitar and just cycle through the same 3 or 4 things you've been playing for months until you get tired or bored?

…spend your entire practice session watching YouTube videos the whole time and not playing a single note?

…spend all of your practice time studying music theory or ear training drills and you still can't play any songs?

…only play guitar by itself and never with the record?

…practice scales & exercises the entire practice session because you heard that's what you should be doing?

…practice scales, exercises, and/or chords hoping that maybe, one day, it will lead you to playing an actual song?

...want to play songs, but don't think you're ready (or worse, don't think you're worthy)?

...randomly play notes or chords while you watch TV?

If ANY of these sound like how you currently practice, then it's probably not getting you to playing music fast enough...if at all.

You'll be relieved to know there's a MUCH better way to practice that will give you more impressive results with much less work.

DISCLAIMER: I'm not saying you won't need to practice at all. That's just a pipe dream. I'm just saying that the work you do put into guitar will be rewarded every time you practice and you're going to be practicing less than you might think. In fact, you're going to be practicing a lot less...and you'll be playing more music you love because of it.

* * * *

PRACTICING GUITAR VS. PLAYING GUITAR

Practicing Guitar and Playing Guitar are two completely different things and you will need to experience both to make the fastest progress on guitar.

Practicing is all about improving the things you can't play.

Ask yourself, *"What do I suck at?"* or *"What do I not know yet?"* and you'll get a good idea of what you need to practice.

Playing, on the other hand, is when you pick up your guitar and just play effortlessly.

No straining.

No trying to remember whether it's a D Major or a B minor coming up *(that's for Practicing)*.

Playing guitar means you're not working on anything anymore with that particular song.

Your guitar becomes an entertainment centre, a sanctuary, and a playground at the same time.

Practicing is a process.

Playing is a <u>FEELING</u>.

You will experience both Practicing & Playing in each of your Fast Practice Sessions.

And Chapters 5 through 9 will outline exactly how to achieve that.

So you can sit down with your guitar for any amount of time:

- 5 minutes
- 15 minutes

OR EVEN

- One hour

And feel confident you're making steady progress each time.

SONG SELECTION

When it comes to selecting songs for your Fast Practice Sessions, I highly encourage you to select songs you love.

This is especially true if you are still in your first year of learning to play the guitar.

There's really no point learning anything else on guitar other than songs you love.

Unless you're learning a song for a specific purpose (i.e. playing a loved one their favourite song on their birthday), then you'll want to focus exclusively on learning songs YOU love because they will be way more fun to play and you will have a head start with learning them compared to learning a song you've never heard before.

This is because you've already heard the song so many times and have an intimate knowledge of how the song is supposed to sound, including the general flow of chords and the overall structure of the song (i.e. Intro, Verse, Chorus, Verse 2, etc.).

The payoff of playing songs you love is also greater than if you were to play something boring and lifeless like a scale or exercise.

A QUICK NOTE ABOUT SCALES & EXERCISES

Don't get me wrong.

Scales & exercises DO have their purpose for helping you with more advanced applications (i.e. improvising a solo, diving into music theory, shredding, etc.)…

…but until you can play REAL MUSIC on your guitar, you won't need to learn any scales or exercises because the songs you love contain all the lessons & techniques you need.

That's why everything in this book is based on learning how to play guitar THROUGH the songs you love.

If you must insist on practicing scales & exercises (even though I recommend against it right now), then just make sure to ALWAYS practice them in a MUSICAL way such as practicing them over a song in the same key, so you can hear how the notes function with the other instruments.

I'm only including this because I know a lot of people will ask me about it.

I believe the benefit of learning songs far outweighs the benefit of learning scales.

A song is like a delicious meal, ready to eat.

A scale is like ingredients in a bowl, uncooked, with no instructions on how to turn it into a finished meal.

Lots of prep time and no direction.

Learn from the masters who have already done all the work for you and made you your favourite songs.

Play those songs, and I promise your fingers will be able to do everything you want them to do.

Make sense?

Good. Next, we'll talk about the one mindset that will slow you down and prevent you from quickly playing songs on your guitar.

ACTION ITEMS TO INCREASE YOUR SONG PLAYLIST

1. Write the reason why you wanted to learn to play guitar in the first place and make what you wrote visible to you while you're practicing.
2. List 5 songs you would love to play on guitar *(don't over-think this)*.
3. List 3 possible times of day where you can pick up your guitar and play without interruption.

* * * *

MORE READING/LISTENING

Visit **PracticeLessPlayMore.com** for a secret bonus chapter plus a list of recommended resources and additional notes that expand on this topic.

Chapter 2:
Death Of A Perfectionist

On the road to playing your favourite songs on the guitar, you will often encounter A LOT of resistance.

You might have to skip a practice session because the kids are sick...

Or the song you chose has the dreaded F Major chord in it and you still don't know how to play Barre Chords clearly.

Or you're browsing YouTube and you have no idea what video to choose because there are just way too many.

Any one of these can derail your progress and prevent you from achieving your goal on guitar.

However, when it comes to getting rapid results on guitar and playing the songs you love, there's really one common enemy you will encounter along the way and I want to address it now before it creeps in and destroys your progress.

That enemy, my friend, is PERFECTIONISM.

Before we go any further, I need you to ask yourself one important question:

(And be honest with yourself)

Are you a Perfectionist?

If you are not getting the results you want on the guitar and you're reading this book, chances are, you are a Perfectionist.

It's ok, I used to be one too.

Correction.

I'm actually a recovering Perfectionist and I've just built up enough good habits and a lot of good people around me to keep me from falling into that mental trap like I used to.

"Hi, my name is Steve and I'm a Perfectionist."

"Hi Steve."

It's something I have to constantly keep my eye on.

Because that voice in our head telling us "it has to be perfect" is one sassy bitch.

There's really no such thing as perfect anyway.

I've played hundreds of shows in front of audiences as big as 60,000 people and I can honestly say, I've never had a perfect show.

I've made at least one mistake EVERY single time I've performed live.

And I'm ok with it.

When we aim for perfection, we create way too much pressure on ourselves and often end up not even starting.

(Often called "Analysis Paralysis")

This is a great way to Play Less and STRESS More! ;)

PERFECTIONISM'S EVIL TWIN

According to business coach Dan Sullivan, Perfectionism is DIRECTLY tied to procrastination.

Ever have that feeling where you know you should practice, and you may even want to practice, but you just can't bring yourself to get started?

- There's just one more thing to do around the house...
- One more email to check...
- One more episode of Seinfeld you want to watch.

Believe it or not, if you're procrastinating it likely has to do with your need to be perfect.

The goal of each practice session is NOT to play a song perfectly.

That is impossible.

In order to make the kind of rapid progress I outline in this book, it requires you to think differently about how you approach practicing altogether.

The goal of each practice session is to improve 1% or more each time, so you feel like you're making meaningful progress EVERY time you pick up your guitar.

Good luck putting the guitar down when you're getting steady results that you know will only continue.

So if you ever feel Perfectionism rearing its ugly head while you're practicing…

Here are 3 Mantras you can use to immediately stop it in its tracks:

- "Done is better than perfect"
- "Progress over perfection"
- "Play now, polish later"

You can say them out loud three times before and after each practice session.

You can even take a second to say them right now if you want for good measure. ;)

Since making progress, gaining confidence, and creating momentum are the main goals here, we need to structure our practice in a way that kills multiple birds with one stone, so to speak.

That means there's no room for perfectionism and we can't allow ourselves to be too precious about any aspect of playing guitar, including how we practice, when we practice, or what we practice.

What we're aiming for are steady RESULTS.

And as you'll discover in the next chapter, your guitar practice will become all about creating a game you're guaranteed to win every step of the way.

When you can do that, suddenly your attitude about practicing will completely change…

- You will procrastinate less…
- You won't care about the little mistakes anymore…

AND

- You will start to play songs a lot faster because you've removed the pressure and the stress that often comes from wanting to play them perfectly.

I know from experience what it's like to battle the Perfectionist voice in my head.

And what I've found is, the best way to overcome its fury is with steady wins.

So that's exactly what you'll learn how to do in the next chapter…

ACTION ITEMS TO INCREASE YOUR SONG PLAYLIST

1. Pick up your guitar and make a mistake on purpose. Seriously.
2. Write down the 3 mantras and keep them in your practice space where you can see them.
3. For one week, say the 3 mantras 3 times before and after each practice session.

* * * *

MORE READING/LISTENING

Visit **PracticeLessPlayMore.com** for a secret bonus chapter plus a list of recommended resources and additional notes that expand on this topic.

Chapter 3:
How To Create a Game You're Guaranteed To Win

According to Greg McKeown, author of the book *Essentialism*, human beings are motivated most by achievement and recognition of achievement.

In other words, we might want to play our favourite song on guitar for ourselves, so we can say we achieved it…

But according to Greg, it is also incredibly motivating for us when someone hears a song we're playing on guitar and they recognize it right away, telling us it sounds great.

That feeling is priceless.

In order to achieve this scenario, make the fastest progress, and play the song you love on your guitar as soon as day 1…

We need to keep things SIMPLE.

I mean ridiculously simple.

THE K.I.S.S. PRINCIPLE

As you can probably tell from reading this book…

(Or the fact that I wrote a book about practicing at all)

I take a VERY strategic approach to practicing.

I'd rather learn a song once and play it for a lifetime, than be battling the same parts for years through mindless repetition.

Maybe it's all the time I spent alongside Gene Simmons while I was opening for KISS across North America back in 2010 and the influence it had on me…

But I take the K.I.S.S. Principle to heart.

In this case K.I.S.S. stands for Keep It Super Simple.

And what I've found is that the brain works best when everything is kept as simple as possible.

That's how you make steady, predictable progress.

Making steady progress leads to maintaining a solid practice habit, having a higher motivation to pick up the guitar, and ultimately getting faster results.

You're basically creating a game you're guaranteed to win.

What exactly is a game you're guaranteed to win and how do you create one?

The answer to that question lies in another question…

What is the SIMPLEST version of the guitar part you want to play that your brain clearly understands and your fingers can play right away?

- Maybe it means the chords are temporarily converted into simplified versions that require less movement...
- Maybe the Strumming Pattern is removed and you just use Single Strums (*i.e. Downstrokes on each new chord*)...
- Or maybe you don't even play chords at first and just strum along with the record while muting the strings.

There are as many ways to simplify a song as there are songs, so these are just a few examples.

At first, you might need an expert to help you simplify certain guitar parts, but once you get the hang of it, I promise it will become second nature.

You'll instantly be able to find the path of least resistance with every guitar part you want to play.

(This is also a great skill to develop if you're interested in teaching guitar)

You might be wondering why you would want to play a simplified version when you can just try to play what's on the record.

It makes sense why you would think that.

If you've ever tried to learn to play a song you love and the first thing you learn is exactly what you hear on the record, then you know how that process can take forever.

More like Guitar Straining rather than training.

It's possible this approach worked out for you once or twice, but in my experience from coaching over 20,000 guitarists both online & offline for the past 16 years, I know it doesn't really work for most people.

Playing too much too soon overloads the brain and creates too much tension in both your mind and muscles.

Not to mention the frustration it can cause.

Before you chalk it up to "just needing more practice" and blindly believing that it will all work out...

I urge you to consider opening your mind to another possibility where you eat the elephant one bite at a time.

Because if you think about it...

If you aren't able to play the simplified version, then how can you expect to play anything that is more complex?

That's why you play simple versions ASAP

- To get you playing music faster...
- To give you something you feel like you fully own...

AND

- To give you something to easily build on.

It seems like the process will be slower or it will take longer, but once you experience this simple system for yourself, I'm sure you'll agree that it's way faster and way more fun to practice like this.

That's because the key to rapid results is to start small and build momentum.

QUICK TIPS FOR SIMPLIFYING A GUITAR PART

While it's impossible to list all the ways you can simplify a guitar part, here are a few quick tips to get you started:

CHORDS

- Play Barre Chords without trying to barre all 5 or 6 strings (instead, focus on pressing the root note on String 5 or 6 and only playing 3 or 4 strings of the chord clearly)…
- If all the chords in the song are Barre Chords, then play them all on the same string (i.e. String 6)…
- Play Barre Chords as Power Chords first…
- Play Power Chords as just single string root notes (like a bass player would play)…
- If the chords in the song are Open Chords, play simple chords like my "Super Glue Chords" instead…
- If the chords in the song are a mixture of chord families (i.e. Barre Chords, Open Chords, Power Chords, etc.), use a software like Play Along Pal (**PlayAlongPal.com**) to simplify everything to one chord family…
- Use a capo if necessary, to make the chord shapes easier…
- Don't strum and just form the chords with your fretting hand…
- Slow down the song on YouTube or with an app…

STRUMMING & PICKING

- Strum once per chord (Single Strumming)…
- Strum steady Downstrokes to the pulse of the song (Steady Strumming)…
- If you can't play chords while strumming, practice the

Strumming Pattern only and mute the strings with your fretting hand...

- If the guitar part involves a complex picking pattern, strum the chords instead...
- Play a simplified picking pattern (i.e. starting from the root note of the chord and picking each string in the chord, one string per beat)...
- Be reckless with your picking & strumming and don't worry about accuracy for now...

LEAD GUITAR

- Only use your Index Finger to play all notes in the riff/lick/solo...
- Instead of bends, play slides (a half bend = one fret slide, a full bend = two fret slide, a one and a half step bend = three fret slide)...
- remove all legato techniques (bends, slides, hammer-ons, pull-offs, etc.) and pick each note for now...

∗ ∗ ∗ ∗

These are just a few ideas to simplify a song.

There are an endless amount of ways to simplify songs and you will become better & faster at coming up with ways to simplify the more you do it.

Also, you might want to consider hiring a guitar coach or asking an expert to help get you started with simplifying a song.

You can always message me for ideas at **support@rockstarmind.com**

Next, let's take a look at a practical example of simplifying a classic song…

HOW TO PLAY A CLASSIC SONG FROM DAY 1

Let's say your favourite song is "Hotel California" by The Eagles.

It's definitely one of mine.

You might think the opening guitar riff is too complicated to play and it's way beyond your current level of playing.

Or maybe you actually tried to play the riff, got frustrated, and gave up after making the same mistakes over and over again.

The only reason the song was hard to play was because of the approach you took to play it.

Beginner Guitarists tend to take all guitar parts at face value meaning when they learn a new song, they try to play the exact guitar parts they hear on the record right away.

This can result in a painfully slow experience where you learn the first move and then the second move and the third move, etc. in a slow, disjointed way…

…to the point that when you play it all together, what you play barely even resembles the song.

Even worse is when you play it for someone and they don't have the slightest clue what song you're playing.

Especially when you know it's one of their favourites.

Ouch!

It's time to take a different approach to learning songs.

When you start learning a new song on the guitar, you don't need to start by playing the guitar parts exactly as they sound on the record.

You can start by either playing a simplified version of the song and singing on top of it *(if you sing)*...

Or you could play a simplified version along with the record, which you'll see is a strategy I highly recommend adopting.

However, if you're not careful, even this approach can have its pitfalls because you might search for "easy guitar" videos on YouTube and then just take whatever the instructor is saying at face value.

Beginner Guitarist: *"The instructor plays 'Hotel California' with Open Chords and calls it an 'Easy Version'. Let's give it a shot."*

But you'll often find that what experienced guitarists call 'easy' can still be way too difficult to play for a Beginner Guitarist.

So it's no surprise that when you try playing their 'easy' version, you get frustrated when you can't pull off the twisting and the turning right away...

...thinking there's something wrong with you because you can't even play the easy version.

Again, this isn't your fault because many guitar instructors may have forgotten how much coordination is actually involved in playing a song in time on the guitar.

And what they're calling 'easy' isn't easy enough

So if you want to start playing songs on your gu
you just have to stop learning songs at face value
about practicing in a slightly different way.

THE OLD WAY vs. THE NEW WAY

Instead of tackling "Hotel California" like this:

- Trying to play the fingerpicking part you hear on the record
  one note at a time at a snail's pace and going back to the
  beginning every time you make a mistake…

OR

- Trying to play an Easy Version you find on YouTube and
  being on the brink of smashing your guitar when the chord
  switches feel impossible to play.

Instead, I would tackle "Hotel California" like this and create a game
I'm guaranteed to win each step of the way:

Game #1: Find the root notes on String 6 *(B, F#, A, E, G, D, E, F#)*

Game #2: Play each root note and hold for 4 beats *(counting out
loud)*

Game #3: Play root notes along with the Intro on the record

Game #4: Turn notes into Power Chords and play along with the
record

Game #5-8: Turn Power Chords into Barre Chords one string at a
time

: Strum Barre Chords along with the record

ame #10: Play a basic Picking Pattern for each Barre Chord

Etc.

This is just ONE example of how you can simplify the opening riff to "Hotel California".

If there's anything in there that you don't understand, that's ok.

The point of that list is to show you how to create a game you're guaranteed to win every step of the way.

This is exactly how Enrique R. from Nashville tackled "Hotel California".

At first, he hated Barre Chords, but after going through this process...

...well, he still hated Barre Chords, lol.

But he could play them with ease.

IF THE GAME IS TOO DIFFICULT AND YOU CAN'T WIN

The best part about creating games you're guaranteed to win is that whenever you tackle something that is too complicated, you can always fall back on the previous version (*your previous wins*) and enjoy playing those for a little while.

Because everything is musical (and not slow and disjointed)...

You can play up to speed with the record as soon as day 1.

Then just focus on making the next game a little easier than the one you were struggling with.

So you're guaranteed to win.

Remember, you're in control of creating the games the whole time, so always focus on starting as simple as possible and then just stretch your ability bit by bit.

And then watch the magic happen.

Sure, it might seem counter-intuitive to add more steps to learning a new song because it seems like it will take you longer to cross the finish line and play the classic riff.

But think about it for a second...

The "old way" means a potentially gruelling process where actual music (chords & melodies being played to a steady pulse) is never guaranteed to be played.

The "new way" means you're playing real music in every single step.

And once you experience a few wins for yourself...

Wins that come from keeping it super simple and stretching your ability just a little bit each time...

You'll understand how quickly the brain can learn when it is unstressed.

YOUR STRESS METER

I want to close this chapter by quickly talking about stress.

There are two types of stress:

- Good stress (aka "Eustress" - pronounced "YouStress")

AND

- Bad stress (aka "Distress")

Good stress is when we are doing something that isn't too challenging and isn't too easy.

(Like a game we're guaranteed to win)

Bad stress is when we are doing something that is way too challenging for way too long.

(Like practicing the intro to "Hotel California" for weeks without making any noticeable progress)

We all have a Stress Meter inside of us.

Good Stress happens from about level 2-4.

Bad Stress begins at about level 5-7 and becomes super noticeable at level 8-10.

We want to make sure we <u>NEVER</u> get to that point.

Your Stress Meter is how you'll know if you're creating a game you're guaranteed to win or taking on too much too soon.

Are you idling at a healthy 2 or 3 and getting a nice burst of energy when you win each game?

Or are you red lining at 10 or 11 and feeling frustrated because you're playing chord shapes that seem like they require you to have 6 fingers to play clearly?

Your Stress Meter is something you have to continuously monitor when you're practicing if you want to practice less and play more.

Because even if you start your practice session at a 2 or 3…

Your Stress Meter can quickly shoot up to 11 if you're not careful.

(i.e. If you practice for too long, you ate too much pizza earlier and are feeling groggy, or you're going into your practice session with a lot on your mind)

If it does hit 11 (or anywhere close), you know the game you created is too difficult.

You want to keep your Stress Meter idling at 2 or 3…that's what I call your "Stress Sweet Spot".

You'll know when you're in your Stress Sweet Spot when it feels great to practice.

Where you're having fun and feeling confident.

Where you're able to win the game after only one or two tries.

MY EXPERIENCE LEARNING "HOTEL CALIFORNIA" (ON CAMERA)

When you tackle "Hotel California" by trying to play each part on the record up to speed, your Stress Meter can easily hit 11 after even just a few mistakes.

That happened to me when I learned the Intro up to speed in 30 minutes at a recent #PajamaJAM - a show I host where I learn popular riffs & solos LIVE on camera.

The pressure of learning the riff up to speed in under 30 minutes was already enough to make me sweat...

Add a live audience and me talking through everything I'm thinking while I'm practicing *(rather than just practicing in peace)...*

Was a liiiiiittle bit INTENSE!

It was a photo finish to get the opening riff down and I had to make sure that I simplified the parts each step of the way, so I could remain in my Stress Sweet Spot of 2 or 3.

Doing that meant less muscle tension, less mental tension, and greater chances of developing the muscle memory I needed to play the complex guitar part up to speed in only 30 minutes.

* * * *

This was my experience with the song.

You don't need to learn the opening riff to "Hotel California" in 30 minutes.

You don't even need to learn the opening riff at all.

My hope is simply that you now have a better understanding of what goes into playing a new riff quickly.

And the importance of creating a game you're guaranteed to win each step of the way.

The rest of this book will be based on this idea, including how to easily program a practice habit into your life (even if you have a super busy schedule)…

…which is what we'll be talking about in the next chapter.

ACTION ITEMS TO INCREASE YOUR SONG PLAYLIST

1. Pick a song from the list you made in Chapter 1.
2. Write down 3 potential ways you can simplify the song to create your first game you're guaranteed to win. The easier the song the better.
3. Play the guitar part and see if you can win the game.

* * * *

MORE READING/LISTENING

Visit **PracticeLessPlayMore.com** for a secret bonus chapter plus a list of recommended resources and additional notes that expand on this topic.

Chapter 4:
How To Easily Program A New Habit Into Your Life

I'm just going to come right out and say it…

I'm absolutely obsessed with programming new habits into my life and the lives of my students!

Whether it's a guitar practice habit, a fitness habit, or simply remembering to put a glass of water beside the bed so it's there first thing in the morning…

I love the idea of adding new positive habits that get me closer to my goals or replacing bad habits that prevent me from getting there quickly.

Programming new habits means developing automated "mind machines" in a part of the brain called the basal ganglia.

The basal ganglia is like a hard drive that stores your habits.

The coolest part is that, when you have your habit fully programmed as I'll show you in this chapter, your basal ganglia will do all the heavy lifting for you, so you don't have to think about or force yourself to do ANYTHING...

Your habit just kind of takes care of itself because it will feel like it's a natural part of your day.

Contrast that with how many people approach new habits - trying to add too many things at once with good habits, going cold turkey with bad ones, and overwhelming the brain in a way that makes failure almost guaranteed.

New Year's Resolutions are a perfect example of this.

Imagine it's the beginning of the year and you resolve to practice guitar for one hour per day.

No matter what.

Even though you're still recovering from holiday madness and you have a ton of work waiting for you back at the office.

Because you're excited about playing guitar, you might actually get your one hour of practice in every night for a week or two - creating the illusion of a habit.

You feel great, as if nothing can go wrong.

But suddenly, something unexpected gets in the way and breaks your stride such as...

- a new series being released on Netflix...
- the basement flooding...

OR

- one of your guitar strings snapping and you not being able to get out to the store to buy a new set.

An overwhelmed brain is a master at making excuses.

So that's why in this chapter, I'll show you how to work WITH your brain and your current schedule to create a daily practice habit that you actually enjoy programming.

The best part is all you have to do is follow along with the simple instructions and let the system work its magic.

YOUR DAILY PRACTICE HABIT

If you want to become a better Guitar Player and play the songs you love using the method laid out in this book, then I need you to practice the guitar every day.

That's right.

EVERY SINGLE DAY.

I know that some people who read that who aren't currently practicing might be intimidated or even turned off by that idea and close the book right here.

And they would have good reason to do that.

You may have tried to practice every day in the past and it was hard to keep up with.

But I promise if you keep reading, you'll find that programming a new practice habit is not only possible, but it's also very easy to do.

The reason many people don't practice and convince themselves they don't have any time is because...

- They aren't sure what to work on when they sit down to practice...
- They've tried guitar in the past and failed and really don't know how to get a different outcome if they start again...

OR

- They think that they have to practice at least 45-60 minutes per night.

Well, the good news is I never said anything about practicing for 45-60 minutes per night.

I mean, sure, that would be great if you have that kind of time available (especially if you use the method laid out in this book)...

But 45-60 minutes is way too long for what we need to accomplish here.

At least at first.

Because let's be honest.

Our schedules have never been crazier and distractions are at an all-time high.

How many times did something or someone try to get your attention while you read this chapter so far? ;)

So the thought of trying to squeeze in a daily guitar practice habit into an already busy schedule probably isn't the most exciting idea.

What's interesting though is that once you start to see positive results, everything becomes so much easier.

Humans are incredibly motivated by results and we can easily create space in our lives when we associate the activity with progress and fun.

The opposite can be said for things that stress us out (i.e. if we associate guitar with failure because we never got any results).

We sometimes find it hard to even imagine having time in our day when the thing in question stresses us out.

If you aren't currently practicing your guitar every day, you'll be relieved to know that my busiest students are successfully using the technique I'm about to show you to practice every day and make great progress...

...in a completely stress-free way.

I'm still using this technique myself to program new habits into my life *(even habits that aren't related to guitar)*.

DISCLAIMER: This chapter is all about carving out the time to play and not so much about the specific things you will practice in that time *(practice content examples are covered in the chapters that follow)*.

IF YOU'RE ALREADY PRACTICING GUITAR EVERY DAY

If you ARE currently practicing every day...

Then I still want you to read this chapter so you can ensure you are making the most of each practice session and your existing daily habit if you have one.

By following the plan I'm about to lay out, you'll be able to better manage your time while you practice. And depending on your current level of playing, you will even be able to add a new habit to your existing guitar habit *(i.e. learning a new style of music in addition to your regular practice routine).*

So what's the best way to easily program a new habit?

INTRODUCING M.E.D.s

I've found the best, fastest, and easiest way to create a no-fail daily practice habit is to use a technique called M.E.D.s

That stands for "Minimum Effective Dose".

M.E.D.s was first introduced by Nautilus fitness creator Arthur Jones and made famous by lifestyle hacker Tim Ferriss.

I learned it from a Cuban pizza maker back in 2013 lol.

Here's how it works…

You ask yourself: "What is the path of least resistance to produce the desired effect or outcome?"

Or in other words, "What is the easiest way to getting the result I want?"

Originally created for the fitness industry, the Minimum Effective Dose concept has been responsible for people sticking with workout routines long term and seeing amazing results once their new workout habit became a lifestyle habit they didn't need to think about anymore.

For our purposes, you will use the M.E.D.s concept to program a daily guitar practice habit.

You won't be using the New Year's Cold Turkey strategy I mentioned earlier because it isn't reliable since it isn't being fuelled by anything other than excitement.

Once your excitement starts to fade...

Let's say with your first encounter with the B minor chord.

Your habit, and your desire to keep it going, start to fade along with it.

And that's when the excuses start to happen.

"I'll practice after I uhhhh...re-shingle the roof!"

Suddenly the same guitar you were so stoked to play 2 weeks ago gets pushed to the back burner.

AMBITION ALONE CAN'T PROGRAM A HABIT

I remember when I first got serious about playing guitar professionally...

I was 18, fresh out of high school and ready to take on the world with my axe.

The thought of playing guitar all day was a dream come true.

And I was ready to dive right in.

I started by designing a 6 hour per day schedule that would cover every major area of guitar technique:

- Chords
- Strumming
- Leads
- Solos
- Ear Training

AND

- Music Theory

I was unofficially an early investor in Amazon stock for all the books and DVDs I bought.

So the stage was set…

I had everything I needed to become the musician I envisioned.

Every day at 4pm, I would start practicing.

4pm to 6pm would tackle 3 areas, I'd break for dinner, and 8pm to midnight would tackle the remaining 3 areas before going to sleep.

It was perfect, right?

With a schedule like this, there's no way I could fail, right???

Wrong!

Not even close!

Looking back, there are a lot of things wrong with my 6-hour plan.

For the purposes of this chapter, I'll just address the obvious one:

IT WAS 6 HOURS LONG!!!

As stoked as I was to practice and as stoked as I was a few days into it…

The plan was doomed for failure.

It was two weeks into my practice routine and I remember I caught a really nasty cold.

One of those colds that feel like you spent the day in a boxing ring with Tyson.

When the clock struck 4pm, I was still recovering from spending the night building Kleenex Mountain beside my bed.

I was a mess and in no shape to practice.

So I told myself, *"I'll take the day to just flush it out and get back to it tomorrow."*

Believe it or not, I did feel better the next day, so when 4pm rolled around, I went up to my room, sat down at the computer *(where I normally practiced)* and that's when it happened.

I'll never forget that intense feeling of overwhelm when I saw the list of things I needed to practice that day.

What was super exciting just two days earlier was now absolutely terrifying.

The craziest part is that I actually loved practicing and developing my skills as a guitarist.

But the thought of 6 hours was enough for my brain to run at full steam in the other direction.

So I told myself, *"Maybe I just need one more day to get my energy back and I'll come back in full force tomorrow."*

But we both know what happened next.

Just thinking of that list would make me cringe.

I completely lost my drive to practice and it actually took me a little while to recover and get back onto a manageable routine.

This is because I was sold on the idea that anything less than 6 hours would be a waste of time and wouldn't help me achieve my goals.

I took on too much too soon and I got burned for it.

Can you relate?

I know 6 hours sounds extreme *(and it is)*, but a lot of guitarists do the same thing as I did - planning a routine that's completely unmanageable for their schedule - and rely on ambition alone to make it happen.

Well, as you can see from my 6-hour failure, ambition alone can't program a habit.

It was a valiant effort, however…

If I had a hard time forcing a habit at 18 – being a punk kid with no responsibility…

Good luck trying to make it happen now as an adult.

There's just no time to mess around with this stuff.

So that's why you're going to attack the first two crucial weeks of habit programming with the gentlest approach.

Instead of changing your life to fit the guitar…

You're going to change the guitar to fit your life.

This counteracts the natural tendency to get overwhelmed and fill your practice time with another activity…

Thus, killing your momentum.

As you saw from my story, when you skip one day in the first 14 days, skipping more days becomes easier and easier, to the point that it starts to unravel the habit you worked so hard to program.

THE M.E.D.s SCHEDULE

After experimenting with the Minimum Effective Dose technique for over 5 years, I've modified the classic model and made it my own.

The recipe you're about to learn has worked wonders for me across the board, enabling me to:

- play guitar every day
- study 3 languages at the same time
- meditate every morning for 2 years straight
- work out 100 days in a row
- and even write this book

All while managing a chaotic life of touring in a band, being my Dad's primary caregiver, working from home while taking care of my newborn daughter, and running two businesses.

If I can program habit after habit amidst the chaos, then I know you can too.

So let's get to programming!

Here's what your practice schedule will look for the next 30 days:

Phase 1 *(Day 1-14):* Only M.E.D.s
Phase 2 *(Day 14-30):* M.E.D.s + Optional Extra
Phase 3 *(Day 30 and beyond):* Time Stretch + Backup M.E.D.s

Let's dive in…

PHASE 1: ONLY M.E.D.s

In this first phase, your main goal is to practice the bare minimum you can handle.

This could mean only playing a few chords…

Playing a short song…

Or simply just picking up the guitar, strumming all the open strings one time, and then putting it down.

The more ridiculous it seems to you, the better.

You just want to be able to say you picked up the guitar and practiced.

That's what Phase 1 is all about - the bare minimum.

As a general guideline for Phase 1, I recommend picking up the guitar for 5 minutes per day when it's the most convenient for you.

Set a timer for 5 minutes, hit START, and practice whatever you want to practice.

Without ANY worry, care, or self-imposed pressure to do anything in particular.

When the timer goes off, you STOP!!!

That's right, stop playing.

Respect the timer.

I know that might set off alarms and red flags for you.

"5 minutes Steve??? Come on! How am I supposed to play the entire Queen catalogue on guitar if I only practice for 5 minutes per day?!?!?"

Lol. Hold your horses, man!

It's so funny how I usually hear this kind of pushback from the guitarists who don't even have a consistent practice habit going.

It's ok though.

This is a natural response you'll have quite often (especially while reading the upcoming chapters).

Your brain constantly compares new concepts it hears about to widely accepted concepts such as how it's important for you to practice guitar for at least 45-60 minutes per day.

So anything different than that can create mental friction.

Remember, in this first Phase, your ONLY goal is to pick up the guitar and practice something.

If I ask you in 14 days, *"How often do you pick up the guitar?"*

I just want you to be able to say, *"I play every day."*

No need to mention 5-minute timers or bare minimum practice agendas.

The ONLY thing that matters to good ol' basal ganglia is you practiced.

That's it!

Are you seeing where I'm going with this?

If you're practicing guitar every day, then you're effectively telling your brain that practice is something you do daily.

That's when your brain goes to work in the background and does everything it needs to do to support your new habit.

With this in mind, you can probably see why traditional practice methods don't work as well.

They put too much stress on your mind in the first 14 days and make it hard, if not impossible, to build on top of (*i.e. adding more time and practice content to your habit*).

Whereas this method eases into the habit so sneakily…it's almost like a backdoor approach.

It asks you to invest only 14 days of low-stress practice to start forming your new habit and then you gradually build on it from there in Phase 2.

Start the 5-minute timer, practice for 5 minutes, and then stop when you hear the alarm.

Easy peasy.

5 minutes is so simple and I've never met a person who couldn't find 5 minutes per day to practice.

Because if you can't even find 5 minutes per day to practice, then how can you expect to find 45 minutes or more?

That's why we keep it super simple and set a timer for 5 minutes to start.

By the way, an added benefit of stopping as soon as the timer goes off...

I mean actually stopping and putting the guitar down.

(Don't worry guys, it's only 2 weeks)

Is that you build up your DESIRE to practice more...

Because you just stopped short.

It's like taking candy from a baby.

The baby wants what it can't have and can become pretty intense about getting it back.

Instead of dreading practice, you begin to look forward to it.

14 days of a strict 5-minute practice schedule and you'll want to move mountains just to pick up the guitar and practice again.

Try it out!

It's so crazy it just might work! ;)

THE PILLOW TRICK

Before we move on to Phase 2, I want you to meet Rowena, a single mother with 3 jobs, who has been one of my guitar students for over 10 years and is officially the busiest person I know.

When I first met Rowena, she told me how she loved music and she wanted to play guitar, but she was thinking it would be impossible to play because she literally had no time to practice.

I've always loved the Arnold Schwarzenegger quote "You can have results or excuses. Not both."

But come on Arny...

I mean a single mother with 3 jobs???

Now THAT'S a busy schedule and a damn good excuse not to practice!

But Rowena was serious about playing guitar.

So with my M.E.D.s in mind, I thought, *"When is a consistent time in Rowena's day when she could practice? An event that is guaranteed to happen every day that we can just attach guitar practice onto?"*

I went through her entire day and that's when I came up with it.

Bedtime!

Everyone has to go to sleep at some point.

And that's when I came up with something I call "The Pillow Trick".

The Pillow Trick is basically a simple practice hack where you wake up in the morning, put your guitar in the same spot of your bed where you sleep, so at night, when it's time for bed, you have to pick up the guitar in order to sleep…comfortably.

And while your guitar is in your hands, you might as well strum for 5 minutes before putting it down.

Then in the morning when you wake up, you repeat the process…

Guitar goes on the bed…

You pick up the guitar when it's time for bed…

You play for 5 minutes…

You put the guitar down…

Repeat for 14 days.

This is the fail-safe technique for even the busiest of schedules.

If it can help Rowena find time to practice, then it can help you too.

Of course, if you can easily set aside 5 minutes at another time in your day, then you won't need The Pillow Trick, but you will have it there as a backup just in case you need it.

Maybe your schedule isn't as busy as Rowena's, but at least now you know that if you're really struggling to find time to practice, then The Pillow Trick is the easiest way to get through Phase 1 of M.E.D.s.

So that's Phase 1.

Just make sure you pick up your guitar for 5 minutes without any pressure of doing anything perfectly or practicing anything in particular.

The ONLY goal is picking up the guitar and practicing each day.

And if you can't do the 5 minutes, then just make sure you pick up the guitar, strum once, and put it down…

…feeling great that you did.

Seriously.

No need to question the mysteries of the mind.

This stuff works.

No matter how ridiculous it seems.

14 days. Do it. :)

Next, we look at what to do after the first 14 days are complete.

PHASE 2: M.E.D.s + OPTIONAL EXTRA

Believe it or not, if you made it to this point, then you're well on your way to making guitar practice an automatic habit.

You got over the 14-day hump with hopefully little to no resistance!

Now it's time to stretch a bit.

(In case you've spotted the overlap, this approach is the equivalent of creating a game you're guaranteed to win in the arena of habits)

Your goal for the rest of the month is to keep your M.E.D.s going at a bare minimum *(in our example, it's 5 minutes, but it can be whatever you decide works best for you)*.

And now you're ready to add a little bit more to your habit.

Because now your mind can support it.

So here's what I would do in Phase 2:

1) Set a timer for 5 minutes like you did in Phase 1.
2) Pick up the guitar and play anything until the timer goes off.
3) When the timer goes off, now you have a choice of either stopping or continuing for one more round of 5 minutes with the timer.

Because the extra 5 minutes is optional, there's no added pressure, so your mind is still happy for having achieved the first 5.

What should you practice in the next 5 minutes?

You can practice anything you want!

I know that might put you off a little bit.

You're reading this book on practicing and I'm telling you to pick up the guitar and practice anything.

So I don't blame you if you're wondering where I'm going with it.

Here's my logic:

This chapter is one of the first in the book (and one of the longest) for a good reason.

I know how tough it can be for you to program new habits and I really don't think enough emphasis is put on how easy it can be if you just focus on getting your Minimum Effective Dose done in Phase 1…

…without any pressure or preconceived notion of what to do

beyond that.

With the M.E.D.s approach, you are really focusing everything on the understanding that your brain needs time to process things with little to no stress if it's going to quickly give you a habit you can rely on.

M.E.D.s makes your habit feel natural, just something you do in your day, and something that's easy to maintain.

That's how I was able to meditate every morning for 2 years straight, how I'm able to work out 100 days in a row (and counting), and how I was able to start a writing habit that allowed for me to complete this book in under a week.

I like having my basal ganglia automatically do the work for me because that means I just have to show up and practice without ANY resistance.

That's why I invest so much of my time upfront to just showing up and not getting caught up in how much or how little I'm able to practice or what I can play perfectly.

Because I understand that once my habit becomes fully programmed and feeling automatic, I can lengthen my practice sessions as well as expand the practice content very easily.

That's exactly what you'll do in Phase 3.

PHASE 3: TIME STRETCH + BACKUP M.E.D.s

Congratulations on making it to Phase 3!

Now you should be feeling like playing guitar every day in a structured way is something you do naturally.

You have no idea how much further along you are than many guitarists who either own a guitar and don't practice at all, practice sporadically, or guitarists who do play every day, but are just wasting time spinning their wheels.

Your brain is ready to commit to a little more time and that's exactly what you're going to do next.

The optional 5 minutes you added in Phase 2 will be added to your original 5 and your practice sessions will now be 10 minutes long.

Set your timer for 10 minutes, pick up the guitar, and practice anything you want to practice.

Technically, we're still in habit-forming mode, so we don't want to go crazy here, but you can start planning your sessions a bit more now *(using the techniques in the next chapter)* and use your practice time to work on songs you love.

When the timer goes off, stop practicing, and fight any urge to continue practicing in order to let that desire to play guitar grow.

It's a short-term sacrifice for a long-term gain.

Phase 3 will continue until you get that feeling where picking up your guitar to practice is just something that's a part of your day.

Something obvious.

A true lifestyle habit.

EXTENDING M.E.D.s

Now that you know how the M.E.D.s technique works and how it can help you program a new habit, you might be wondering when it's the right time to extend your practice sessions.

If your mind went straight to your Stress Meter, then you're absolutely right!

If you monitor your stress levels, you can adjust your practice time accordingly.

So if you practice for 10 minutes one day, you get on a roll and you want to continue for another hour, it's totally fine.

As long as you complete your MINIMUM time of 10 minutes, you're good.

This is different than just jumping into an hour-long session.

In this example, you are still thinking of practicing for only 10 minutes and once that's completed, you can continue practicing because you're enjoying yourself.

Then tomorrow might be a busy day where all you can do is your 10 minutes Minimum Effective Dose.

That's the beauty of M.E.D.s.

Once you're in Phase 3, you're only required to get your minimum practice time in and then you can do whatever you want after that.

And if/when life gets crazy and you can't get your full practice time in...

…then just focus on getting in your bare minimum, so you can keep your momentum going until life settles back down and then you can ramp things back up.

It's WAY easier to move forward in a vehicle that's already moving (even slowly) than it is to start moving one that is stopped.

So the idea is to never stop your daily habit.

Instead, you will keep it going throughout the chaos and the calm, adjusting how much you do each day.

Make sense?

* * * *

When deciding how to stretch your M.E.D.s practice time from 10 minutes to 15 and beyond…

As a general rule, I recommend adding 5 minutes approximately every 2 weeks.

Start with the optional 5 minutes at the end of your session and then add the 5 minutes to the original time for two weeks.

If you follow this model exactly and your goal is to eventually practice guitar for 20 minutes per day, then it would look something like this:

Day 1 - 14 = 5 minutes
Day 14 - 30 = 5 minutes + optional 5
Day 30 - 45 = 10 minutes
Day 45 - 60 = 10 minutes + optional 5
Day 60 - 75 = 15 minutes

Day 75 - 90 = 15 minutes + optional 5

After a couple of months, you can probably stretch your M.E.D.s by more than just 5 minutes at a time and progress faster than the example schedule above.

But that's for you to decide.

Always rely on your Stress Meter to guide you.

If adding more minimum practice time adds stress in ANY way, then it isn't the right time to add it.

I'd rather you took 90 days to have a rock-solid habit of 20 minutes per day, than practicing for 20 minutes too soon and not being able to maintain it.

And remember, you always have the original M.E.D.s to fall back on as a backup.

If you build up your practice habit to 15, 20, or even 30 minutes of practice per day and then one day, something keeps you from going through your routine, then no problem.

Simply pick up your guitar, strum once and put it down again like you did in Phase 1.

And just pick up where you left off when you practice tomorrow.

That's how we keep the momentum going.

All we care about in these early stages is <u>THAT</u> you're playing every day and not WHAT you're playing every day.

Know what I mean?

We'll discuss examples of what you can practice in the following chapters.

YOUR WINNING STREAK

Now that you know the 3 Phases of M.E.D.s, you might be wondering the best way to keep track of your brand-new habit.

It's just as important to see that you're making progress as it is to actually make the progress itself.

So I've found the most powerful way to keep track of your habit as you're programming it is using something I call a Winning Streak.

You basically have 30 boxes on a sheet of paper (or a calendar) and you mark a single X in the day's box every time you complete your practice session.

- If you pick up your guitar and strum, you mark an X…
- If you pick up your guitar and play the first three chords to "Free Fallin'", you mark an X…

AND

- If you pick up your guitar and strum as fast as you can for 10 minutes, you mark an X.

You get the picture.

This simple Winning Streak strategy is based on a method made popular by none other than Jerry Seinfeld.

Seinfeld uses this method to write new jokes and material for his show every day *(and we all know how well that worked out for him)*.

Here is his advice for being super productive and getting MASSIVE results in your art:

"After a few days you'll have a chain. Just keep at it and the chain will grow longer every day. You'll like seeing that chain, especially when you get a few weeks under your belt. Your only job next is to not break the chain. Don't break the chain."

I like this approach a lot because it makes programming a habit feel like a game.

I'm a super competitive guy, so when I see a few boxes marked with an X, I will do whatever it takes to keep the chain going…

Almost like getting a high score lol.

GOING HORIZONTAL

I always say, "Go Horizontal rather than Vertical."

What that means is it's more important to practice for more days than it is to practice for more time on ONE random day.

When you pick up your guitar every day with M.E.D.s and expose your mind & fingers to the fretboard, you will be able to learn songs faster and remember them for longer because the details are always top of mind.

That means practicing 5 minutes per day is better for you in the long run than practicing 35 minutes once per week.

When coupled with the practice strategies in the upcoming chapters, your solid new practice habit will create the space that guarantees you're able to play the songs you love.

Now that the mental aspects are out of the way, it's time to prep the materials for your first Fast Practice Session.

We achieve that with a process called Pre-Practice, which is the focus of the next chapter.

ACTION ITEMS TO INCREASE YOUR SONG PLAYLIST

1. Choose a time to practice from the list that you made in Chapter 1.
2. Decide how you will track your Winning Streak (i.e. a calendar, a sheet of paper, an app, etc.). The easier the better.
3. Practice for 5 minutes today and mark an X on your Winning Streak once your practice session is done.

* * * *

MORE READING/LISTENING

Visit **PracticeLessPlayMore.com** for a secret bonus chapter plus a list of recommended resources and additional notes that expand on this topic.

Chapter 5:
Pre-Practice

Now that you've programmed a reliable daily practice habit into your life, it's time to discuss two things:

1) WHAT to practice to align with your goals.

AND

2) HOW to practice songs in the least amount of time possible, so you can play it effortlessly ASAP.

This chapter will take care of the WHAT and the entire next section of the book (Part 2: PRACTICE) will take care of the HOW.

WHAT IS PRE-PRACTICE?

You might look at the title of this chapter and wonder, *"Steve, what the Hell is Pre-Practice???"*

And you'd have a good reason to ask that question.

I think you've come to expect from me so far that I like to do things in a different way; a way that doesn't put any negative stress or overwhelm on the brain; a way that keeps our Stress Meter idling at a healthy 2-4 (the Stress Sweet Spot).

Pre-Practice is a natural extension of that.

It isn't as efficient or productive to just pick up your guitar and jump right into practicing.

When you do that, you're often guessing what you should practice next and needlessly taking up precious time while you search for materials to use.

That could lead to unproductive sessions where you finish and feel like you just wasted your time.

Not cool.

Instead, you'll get better results when you add Pre-Practice to the mix.

In a nutshell, Pre-Practice is taking care of all the things you need to prepare for your practice session BEFORE your practice session begins.

The idea is that if everything is ready for you when you sit down to practice, you'll be able to focus 100% on whatever it is you're practicing.

This would be the equivalent of getting your workout clothes ready by the door the day before your workout.

That way, when it's time to work out, all you have to do is grab the clothes and head out to the gym…

…removing any resistance to completing the task at hand.

Pretty cool, right?

This is especially helpful if you only have 10 minutes to practice and need to make the most of that time.

Pre-Practice is typically introduced in Phase 3 of your M.E.D.s Practice Habit and it includes the following:

- Setting your Top Priority Task (TPT)
- Hunting & Gathering practice material
- Quickly Scanning the content
- "Onramping" your equipment for your session

AND

- Any extras you think will make today's session successful

Let's look at each component in detail...

SETTING YOUR TOP PRIORITY TASK (TPT)

First things first.

In order to make the fastest progress possible on the guitar that aligns with your goals, you need to get your priorities straight.

So that means you first want to decide what it is you want to achieve in the first place.

I like to think in 90-day increments.

What result would make you the happiest if you achieved it in the next 90 days?

Another way to think about it would be, if we were talking 90 days from now, what would you love to say you were able to accomplish?

From there you can set everything up to be aligned with that goal.

In Pre-Practice, you will write down the single most important thing you will work on in your next practice session.

This is your Top Priority Task.

Your TPT.

In other words, your Top Priority Task is the main focus of your practice session that as long as you get that one thing done, you can go to bed at night feeling satisfied and accomplished.

At first, you'll probably set vague TPTs like "Play guitar" or TPTs that are way too ambitious for the time you have available like "Learn both solos to 'Sultans Of Swing'".

No worries.

Just go with it for now and try to be as specific & realistic as possible.

You will repeat this process each day and build on what you accomplished in the previous day's practice session.

After about a week, setting a specific & realistic TPT that moves you closer and closer to the finish line will become second nature.

Always try to phrase your TPT with an ACTION and then a SPECIFIC TOPIC.

Here are a few examples of specific TPTs:

- Play first half of "Wish You Were Here" Intro at 70% speed
- Learn Chord Progression to "Twist and Shout"

- Play along with "Dust In The Wind" at full speed

If you're ever stuck trying to figure out what your TPT is for the day, think about what BIGGER GOAL you want to achieve, such as playing someone you love their favourite song, or jamming with your buddies next month.

That will help you choose "Learn the Intro to 'Wonderful Tonight'" as your TPT for the first goal and "Improvise for 5 minutes over "Stairway To Heaven" using the Am Pentatonic Scale" as your TPT for the second.

HUNTING & GATHERING

Now that you have your TPT set and you know what you want to achieve in your upcoming practice session, it's time to gather all the practice materials you will use when you're actually practicing.

That could include searching YouTube for the song or section of the song you want to play (i.e. "Landslide guitar lesson", "we are the champions guitar solo lesson", "how to play Hot For Teacher guitar riff", etc.) and bookmarking any tutorial videos you'll watch.

You can also go to Google and search for TABs, chord diagrams, or lyric sheets (i.e. "Here Comes the Sun guitar chords", "purple haze intro tab", "Space Oddity lyrics", etc.) and bookmark any links you find on sites like Ultimate Guitar or AZ Lyrics.

You can also print them off if you prefer a hard copy.

Go with whatever works best for you.

Remember, you don't have to go crazy getting every single resource imaginable.

Only gather what you need for today's session.

IMPORTANT: ALWAYS take the info you find online with a grain of salt.

It doesn't matter how professional a piece of content looks…

FREE & even paid content is just ONE person's interpretation of how the song should be played on the guitar and sometimes the TAB, chord diagrams, lyrics, or even video lesson can sound WAY off from the original record.

I'm not talking about easy guitar versions where some notes, chords, or strumming are boiled down to the basics…

I'm talking about where it sounds like a completely different song.

This is why learning songs you love is so crucial.

Since you know what the song is supposed to sound like, you'll be able to spot right way if the video tutorial or TAB looks or sounds a bit whacky, and then you can find another source to use.

After a week or so, it should only take you a few minutes to gather the material. And just like with setting your Top Priority Task, it will only get easier to find what you need with time.

If you're working on a song that takes a few days to play, and you've already downloaded the full TAB, then you won't need to gather anything today since you'll likely just re-use the material you gathered before.

Just make sure it's easily accessible for today's practice session.

QUICKLY SCANNING THE CONTENT

Scanning is a crucial step because it means taking the practice material you just gathered and getting a bird's-eye view on it, so you limit any surprises in your practice session.

You will quickly scan through the part(s) you've selected as your TPT for the day and spot any chords/techniques it requires you to play (i.e. hammer-ons, slides, Bm Barre Chord, etc.)

Circle any chords/techniques you don't yet know how to play and mark any section that seems like it might be a problem area.

Scanning also involves watching any tutorial videos you've found in the hunting phase if you have time.

You can even do this at 1.5x or 2x speed to save time by quickly seeing what the tutorial video entails and deciding if it is useful.

Most video players have this speed feature (including YouTube).

This is another opportunity for you to spot "Bad TABs" or video lessons where the only thing that is accurate about the song is the title of the video.

"ONRAMPING" YOUR EQUIPMENT

The coolest part about Pre-Practice is it can happen at different times throughout the day.

As long as it's before you actually practice, you will experience the benefits.

Onramping means setting up your equipment beforehand so you

don't have to go searching for it when you're sitting down to practice.

(Kind of like Hunting & Gathering for equipment)

Onramping can include any of the following:

- Having your picks and capo laid out and easily accessible…
- Taking your guitar out of the case…
- Pre-Tuning your guitar…
- Loading up the song you're learning on Spotify…

OR

- Having your timer pre-set to 5 or 10 minutes

(The Pillow Trick was a simple form of onramping)

EXTRAS

The last component of Pre-Practice is to take care of any extras you think will help your practice session be a smooth one.

That can include both non-guitar equipment and things you need to prepare mentally so your practice session is a success.

Some things that have worked for my students are:

- Having a water bottle or other beverage available for hydration…
- Having a notepad and pen handy to take notes…
- Having your calendar or Winning Streak app easily accessible…
- Saying the Strumming Pattern of the song out loud on the

drive home…

- Singing along with the song you're going to practice today…
- Writing down a chord diagram from the song to help internalize it…
- Writing down the Verse lyrics by hand so you remember them…

AND

- Listening to the song, and taking note of anything you hear that might help you learn the song faster (*i.e. the drummer plays 4 stick clicks before the band comes in, the vocals start on the one beat, etc.*).

Go with what works for you and you'll find that the more you Pre-Practice, the better (and faster) you'll get at preparing all the right components for your upcoming Fast Practice Session.

A QUICK NOTE ABOUT PRACTICE CONTENT

So now that you know what Pre-Practice consists of, I want to show you a few examples of Pre-Practice in action.

While I can't cover every single possibility of what to practice, I will use as many examples as I can.

If you have any specific questions for me about what you should be practicing to achieve your 90-day goal on guitar, then please reach out to me at **support@rockstarmind.com** and I'll be happy to discuss it with you.

PRE-PRACTICE IN ACTION

In order for the Pre-Practice concept to really stick, I think it will be helpful for you to see practical examples of Pre-Practice in action.

That way you can take some of these ideas to use in your own Pre-Practice as soon as today:

EXAMPLE #1

You're a Beginner Guitarist who has been playing acoustic guitar for just over one year.

You know a few chords, but Barre Chords have become your sworn enemy.

You work 9am-5pm in an office downtown and your drive is about 45 minutes with traffic.

You've been practicing for 10 minutes per day at 8pm - after dinner when you can get some quiet time to yourself.

Your favourite band is The Eagles and you've always wanted to play Hotel California.

You love singing the song on your drive to work and you're thinking about performing it at an Open Mic this summer.

It's your first time playing the song, so your Top Priority Task is to learn the first few chords of the Intro.

You print a couple of TABs and watch a quick tutorial on how to play an easy version of the Intro.

You take note of any chords you don't yet know how to play by circling them in red on the TAB sheet you printed.

You've already laid out a couple of picks and a bottle of water by your guitar and will be using your phone as a timer.

You're ready to rock!

EXAMPLE #2

You just started playing guitar and bought a used electric guitar online.

You want to learn Classic Rock tunes by your favourite bands and you just saw a Tom Petty and the Heartbreakers tribute band live last Friday, so you're inspired to get going.

You work from home and set aside some time before lunch to program your practice habit.

Your Pre-Practice consists of tuning your guitar and watching a tutorial video on Free Fallin' while you wait for an email to arrive.

You take a screenshot of the chord diagram for the first chord of the song - D Major - and you get your capo ready for your practice session.

Your TPT is to learn the D chord with the capo on Fret 3.

EXAMPLE #3

You've been playing guitar off and on for about 30 years.

Your son tells you about the Guns N' Roses concert he saw this summer and the two of you watch a few videos of the show he shot on his iPhone.

Hearing the opening riff to "Sweet Child O' Mine" reignites your spark for guitar and you're inspired to dust off the old Les Paul Standard.

You're retired, so setting aside some time for guitar isn't a big deal at the moment.

You used to know how to play the riff, so your TPT is to re-learn all the notes of the opening riff and play it at 50% speed with the record.

You have an old Appetite For Destruction Songbook that you pull out, open to the right page, and put on the music stand.

It still has all your notes scribbled on it, so you quickly scan through those to spot any potential problem areas before you encounter them.

You have a stopwatch on your desk and you'll use it to time the practice session.

WHEN TO PRE-PRACTICE

As you can probably tell from the previous examples, the best part about Pre-Practice is you can perform it without a guitar ANYWHERE and at ANYTIME.

It all depends what you're practicing that day and how much Pre-Practice you need to achieve it.

And it could take up to 10 minutes or it can take as little as 10 seconds.

It's just important that you Pre-Practice so you set yourself up for success when it's time to practice.

Pre-Practice can happen right before you sit down to practice, in between meetings at the office, or even while waiting in line at the bank.

Since a lot of Pre-Practice can be done on your phone, you will want to look for any "Dead spots" in your day where you aren't doing anything productive and you can fill the time with any of the 5 Pre-Practice components mentioned in this chapter.

CONCLUSION TO PART 1

While Pre-Practice isn't mandatory, I highly recommend using it to save yourself from wasting time & energy deciding "on the fly" what to do during the actual practice session itself.

With a little bit of time devoted to Pre-Practice, you will be able to focus 100% of your time & energy on actually achieving your TPT, which is super important when you only have 10 minutes per day to practice.

Now that you've primed yourself with the right mindset to practice less and play more…

…and you have your Pre-Practice material ready…

It's time to discuss HOW you're actually going to practice the material to achieve the fastest result possible.

That's the focus of the next section.

ACTION ITEMS TO INCREASE YOUR SONG PLAYLIST

1. List 3 "Dead spots" in your day where you can Pre-Practice.
2. Write down your goal for the next 90 days.
3. Write down your Top Priority Task for today's Practice session that's aligned with your 90-day goal.

* * * *

MORE READING/LISTENING

Visit **PracticeLessPlayMore.com** for a secret bonus chapter plus a list of recommended resources and additional notes that expand on this topic.

PART 2: PRACTICE

DISCLAIMER!

Before we get into Part 2: PRACTICE, did you read Part 1: PRIME?

Part 2: PRACTICE was designed to build on the mindsets & strategies outlined in the previous chapters, so if you skipped Part 1: PRIME, I strongly urge you to go back and read that section before reading this one.

Your mind is responsible for making the whole PRACTICE LESS, PLAY MORE! system run smoothly.

When your mind fully understands the ins & outs of guitar practice as outlined in this book, it will be able to better control your fingers, help you learn songs faster, and remember songs for longer.

That's why it's so important you start by priming your mind by reading Part 1 first.

And if you've already read Part 1: PRIME, then let's continue…

Chapter 6:
Play BEFORE You Practice

Your Fast Practice Session is about to begin.

You sit down with your guitar; all of your Pre-Practice materials are ready to go for you.

You tune up your guitar up and you're ready to dive right in and start working on the song.

And that's exactly what you should do, right?

Not quite.

Before you dive in and start learning a song, it's important that you start your Fast Practice Session with PLAY.

As you read in Chapter 1 *(you read Chapter 1, right?)*, the guitar is meant to play music, so that's really the focus of this first phase of practice.

And if you remember *(because you totally read that Chapter, right?)*, Playing guitar is very different from Practicing guitar.

Practicing is all about improving the things you can't play.

Playing is when you pick up your guitar and just play effortlessly.

No trying to muscle through a Barre Chord or bend.

No speed drills or pentatonic licks.

Just pure PLAY.

It might seem odd to you that we are starting our practice session with play.

However, in a book called "PRACTICE LESS, PLAY MORE!" It should come as no surprise that playing is the main focus.

So what that means is before you practice, I want you to play something that feels effortless to play.

This is important for so many reasons.

You are Tuning your mind and muscles to play without ANY straining.

Just a peaceful, easy feeling.

And you want to play something that is fun.

So this is the perfect opportunity to quickly play a riff or a section of a song you know.

Maybe it's a little bit of "Black Magic Woman"…

Maybe it's the opening riff to "Satisfaction" by The Stones…

No matter what it is, playing something easy will also act as a great warmup for your fingers and get your mind focused on playing before you dive into practice.

IF YOU DON'T KNOW HOW TO PLAY ANY SONGS

If you're just starting out on guitar or you've been struggling to play anything that sounds like music, then not to worry.

I still want you to play something effortless at the beginning of your session.

Play a single chord that's easy for you *(i.e. an E5 Power Chord)* and strum it wildly like you're an 8-year-old who had too much birthday cake for breakfast.

And if you don't know any chords, then just crank up one of your favourite tunes on Spotify and strum wildly to that...

...without caring that you're playing a ton of wrong notes.

The key here is to set a precedent for that effortless feeling you're experiencing.

Because that's how you want everything you practice to feel once it's fully developed.

HOW LONG SHOULD YOU PLAY BEFORE YOUR FAST PRACTICE SESSION BEGINS?

Playing something easy before your Fast Practice Session begins should only take up the equivalent of 10% of your practice session.

Just a quick little calibration for you before diving in.

No playing Stairway To Heaven and Bohemian Rhapsody in their entirety, ok?

That works out to 30 seconds of playing before a 5-minute Practice Session and 1 minute before a 10-minute Practice Session.

Set your timer and let 'er rip.

When the alarm goes off, you are ready to start your Fast Practice Session.

You'll be playing again at the end of your practice session, so while this short Playing phase is supposed to feel fun, it's also functional - part of a larger system.

Remember to always keep the guitar parts super simple (K.I.S.S. Principle) and play something that's really easy for you to play.

This is not the time to work out any guitar parts.

The goal is simply to tap into that effortless feeling, so you set the stage for everything you're about to practice.

That's about it for this chapter.

Short and sweet like this first Playing phase of your guitar practice plan.

Next, we dive into the meat and potatoes of the book, where you'll learn the same three-step system I'm using to learn songs up to speed in 30 minutes or less on my LIVE #PajamaJAM.

And the same system my students are using to learn an average of 2-3 songs per week on their guitars.

ACTION ITEMS TO INCREASE YOUR SONG PLAYLIST

1. Double check your guitar is in tune.
2. Set a timer for 10% of the duration of your upcoming Fast Practice Session.
3. Play effortlessly until the alarm goes off.

* * * *

MORE READING/LISTENING

Visit **PracticeLessPlayMore.com** for a secret bonus chapter plus a list of recommended resources and additional notes that expand on this topic.

Chapter 7:
The Fast Practice Session

If you've made it this far into the book, read through the previous chapters, and started incorporating the techniques I've shared with you…

Then you are SO far ahead of most guitarists I meet who are learning to play guitar and don't have any idea about how or what they should be practicing.

You now know…

- You must always keep music the main focus…
- The songs you learn should align with your bigger goals (i.e. Bucket List)…
- You must create a game you're guaranteed to win each step of the way…
- You can and should program a daily practice habit to experience the fastest progress on guitar…

AND

- You can give yourself a head start each time you practice with Pre-Practice.

Among other things.

Now it's time to get into the nitty gritty of the book.

I'm about to show you the same three-step system I'm using to learn songs up to speed in 30 minutes or less LIVE on camera *(as seen on my weekly #PajamaJAM that I broadcast on Facebook).*

A QUICK NOTE ABOUT PRACTICE CONTENT

It is out of the scope of the book to show you EVERY possible song and situation you'll encounter and all the ways you can simplify it, since that book would be endless.

What I WILL do is show you how to approach as many situations as possible by including as many song examples as I can.

If my students are any indication…

Once you see me go through the Fast Practice Session and explain how everything works, it will become easier and easier for you to incorporate it into your own practice sessions.

In other words, first I'll catch the fish for you and then once you learn the system, you'll know how to catch fish any time you want.

That way you can learn to play songs you love on guitar pretty much on demand.

And if you're really feeling stuck, you can always message me at **support@rockstarmind.com** to figure out the simplest way to get started.

YOUR FIRST FAST PRACTICE SESSION

Your first Fast Practice Session will be interesting to say the least. ;)

If you've practiced the conventional way of trying something over and over until you get it, then the pace of a Fast Practice Session is very different to what you might have experienced before.

There's no rote memorization or mindless repetition.

It's an extremely flexible process that adjusts to your needs each time you practice.

Below are the 3 main steps of a Fast Practice Session.

We will first describe each element and then I'll show you a real-world example of a Fast Practice Session.

Sound good?

Ok, let's get started.

A Fast Practice Session consists of 3 simple steps:

Step #1 - No Tempo Practice

Step #2 - Slow Tempo Practice

AND

Step #3 - The Fast Practice Formula

STEP #1 - NO TEMPO PRACTICE

Inspired by Jamie Andreas at Guitar Principles and by a festival I played in Indonesia called 1,000 Bands United where each band's start time was so much later than what was originally promised by promoters it made time feel "Elastic"…

I'd like to introduce you to No Tempo Practice.

No Tempo Practice is a powerful addition to your practice toolbox because it allows you to scan through practice materials like TABs & chord diagrams with your guitar while keeping complete control of your mind & fingers the entire time.

No tempo means practicing guitar parts without a steady pulse.

Depending on the song you're learning and your current skill level on guitar, some parts might be a little slower and some a little faster and you should play it at a comfortable speed that feels totally under control.

If it doesn't, then it either means you're going too fast or the guitar part you're trying to play requires more attention.

Take note of this part with a pen or highlight the screen and you will return to it shortly.

Chances are, at first when you attempt No Tempo Practice, you will play way too fast and that's ok.

The discipline to play super slow and adjust the speed based on comfort will take some time to get used to.

Allow yourself to play slowly, knowing it will help you progress faster.

The purpose of No Tempo practice is to actually EXPERIENCE the guitar parts rather than only scanning over them like you did in Pre-Practice.

In Pre-Practice your eyes scanned the practice material and spotted any potential trouble areas.

Now in No Tempo Practice, your fingers actually experience the practice material and spot any trouble areas based on actual physical obstacles you encounter.

Keep your No Tempo Practice short - 2 minutes or less - and only focus on scanning through the section(s) tied to your Top Priority Task.

You only have to complete No Tempo Practice once per Fast Practice Session *(especially when your practice sessions are less than 30 minutes long)*.

I've included examples of No Tempo Practice later in this chapter as well as in the Book Resources page online.

STEP #2 - SLOW TEMPO PRACTICE

Next up is Slow Tempo Practice, which is like No Tempo's cousin.

Slow Tempo is where you practice slowly along with a steady pulse.

Like No Tempo, only in musical time.

In order for Slow Tempo practice to work best, you need to work with a metronome or a slowdown software/app.

Slow Tempo also requires you to work with small sections of your practice material called "Chunks".

A Chunk is a little piece of music that is easy for your mind to understand and your fingers to execute.

This is your first game you're guaranteed to win.

It can be a single chord, a few notes in a riff, an entire bar of music, etc.

As long as it's relatively short and easily manageable, it is a valid Chunk.

And your first Chunk can come from any part of the song (Intro, Verse, Chorus, Solo, etc.) - whatever part is your favourite - although, at first, I recommend you start with the Intro until you complete at least 2 weeks of Fast Practice.

Imagine your Top Priority Task for today is to play the Power Chord riff of "Smells Like Teen Spirit".

Your first Chunk might consist of the Power Chord on Fret 1 of String 6 with the Strumming Pattern "Down UpDown".

So what you would do is play that slowly ONLY ONCE.

I'm talking REALLY slow.

I'm talking SO slow you can't possibly make a mistake.

This is textbook Slow Tempo Practice.

Unlike No Tempo Practice, Slow Tempo Practice actually has a steady pulse to it.

Albeit super slow.

If you played the Chunk correctly, then congratulations!

You're ready for the next step.

If you didn't play the Chunk correctly, then you played it too fast.

Remember, the only requirements of Slow Tempo Practice are that you play with a steady pulse and you play so slow you can't make a mistake.

That means WAY slower that you are currently thinking. ;)

(Sometimes even slower than you would with No Tempo Practice)

Go with whatever speed you need to play the part correctly.

As I mentioned earlier, give yourself permission to play slowly, knowing it's going to help you progress faster.

It may be tough for you to play slowly because you might feel like playing this slowly will mean you always play this slowly, however, that's not the case.

(Quite the opposite actually)

Your mind & muscles work really well with slow tempos and it's widely accepted amongst experienced players that in order to play fast, you need to practice slow.

Practicing slow is an essential part of learning something new, no matter if you're a Beginner Guitarist or a seasoned professional.

So go ahead and practice your first Chunk at a speed that's so slow you can't make a mistake.

Similar to No Tempo Practice, you only have to practice this Chunk ONE TIME.

If you only practiced with No Tempo & Slow Tempo Practice, you would definitely make some progress, however the real magic comes from the next step which is the Fast Practice Formula.

STEP #3 - THE FAST PRACTICE FORMULA

If No Tempo Practice & Slow Tempo Practice are like starting the car and putting it into gear…

…then the Fast Practice Formula is like the steering wheel allowing you to adjust to road conditions ahead as you "drive".

It is what you do with the first Chunk you just played in the previous section and every Chunk from here.

And just like driving, it's all about movement, so one of the best features of the Fast Practice Formula is that you're either adding on each Chunk or simplifying it.

Contrast that to the practice trap of practicing the same guitar part over and over and risking over-practicing.

Over-Practicing is when guitarists practice the parts they successfully develop, keep practicing them instead of moving on, and actually make the parts they develop worse.

the Fast Practice Formula prevents over-practicing because you're always in motion, knowing exactly what to practice next.

Here is the Fast Practice Formula (explanations will follow):

3xWMM = Move On

→ + Speed
→ + Amount
→ + Complexity

2MR = Go Back

← - Speed
← - Amount
← - Complexity

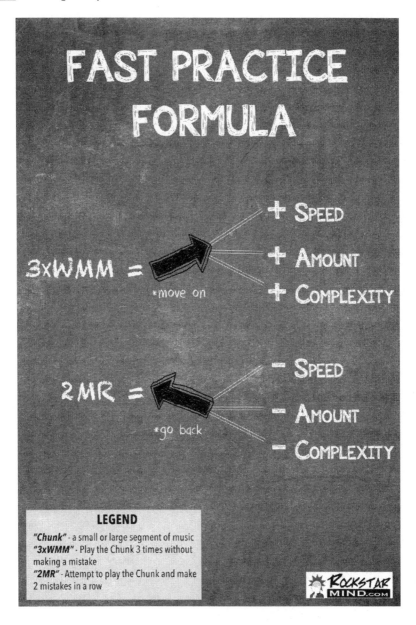

Right now, you might be thinking…

"Ummm, Steve? What the Hell is that thing???"

"That looks like something I left back in my High School science class."

"How is that going to help me play Zeppelin IV in its entirety???"

And so on.

Trust me, this little formula is SUPER powerful and will help you make smart decisions about what to practice each step of the way, so you can cross the finish line in a fraction of the time of conventional practice methods.

First, I'll break down each component of the Fast Practice Formula and then I'll show you some real-world examples:

Formula: 3xWMM = Move On

Definition: Play the current Chunk the same way (same tempo, same Strumming Pattern, chord fingering, etc.) **three times without making a mistake - 3xWMM** (with pauses in between each attempt) before moving on.

Moving on to what?

Moving on to the next level of difficulty.

Here's how:

Modifiers:

$\boxed{\rightarrow}$ + Speed
$\boxed{\rightarrow}$ + Amount
$\boxed{\rightarrow}$ + Complexity

Definition: The next level of difficulty will either consist of:

- practicing the current Chunk faster (3-5bpm faster)

OR

- practicing a different Chunk (i.e. next bar of music)

OR

- adding more notes to the current Chunk (i.e. the next couple of notes in a bar)

OR

- increasing the complexity of the current Chunk (i.e. if you started with a basic Strumming Pattern you can make the next Chunk more complex by adding more strokes to the pattern)

It's your choice.

Each of the 3 Modifiers (Speed, Amount, Complexity) takes the Chunk you just played and stretches your ability just a little bit to create a new game you're guaranteed to win.

Any of the 3 Modifiers will inch you closer and closer to your goal.

Choose one Modifier to create your next Chunk.

There is no wrong answer as long as you don't stretch too much and overwhelm yourself.

Monitor your Stress Meter and make sure you're always idling at a 2-4 (your Stress Sweet Spot).

Let's continue with the second half of the Fast Practice Formula...

What happens when you can't play the Chunk three times without making a mistake.

Formula: 2MR = Go Back

Definition: You made **two mistakes in a row - 2MR -** attempting to play the current Chunk (with pauses in between each attempt), so now you need to go back.

Go back where?

Go back to a lower level of difficulty.

Here's how:

Modifiers:

⬅ - Speed
⬅ - Amount
⬅ - Complexity

Definition: A lower level of difficulty will either consist of:

- practicing the current Chunk slower (3-5bpm slower)

OR

- removing notes from the current Chunk (*i.e. cutting the Chunk in half*)

OR

- decreasing the complexity of the current Chunk (i.e. if you started with Barre Chords, you can make the next Chunk less complex by playing Power Chords)

It's your choice.

Each of the 3 Modifiers (Speed, Amount, Complexity) takes the Chunk you tried to play and simplifies it to increase your chances of playing it three times without making a mistake (3xWMM).

Any of the 3 Modifiers will inch you closer and closer to your goal.

Choose one Modifier to create your next Chunk.

There is no wrong answer as long as you don't stretch too much and overwhelm yourself.

Monitor your Stress Meter and make sure you're always idling at a 2-4 (your Stress Sweet Spot).

Making mistakes is part of learning how to play guitar.

There's no avoiding it.

That's why the Fast Practice Formula exists.

Because it's very easy to select a Chunk that's too fast, too long, or too complex to play three times without making a mistake.

So instead of guessing or over-practicing, you'll make two mistakes in a row (2MR) and know right away that you need to modify your Chunk to something that's easier for you to play.

Use the Fast Practice Formula every day to tackle your Top Priority Task and watch the results start to happen.

Soon you'll be able to select high quality Chunks and develop better practice instincts in real-time...

...just like I do on each episode of #PajamaJAM where I learn a popular riff or solo up to speed in 30 minutes or less LIVE on camera.

Until then, just focus on internalizing the Fast Practice Formula and making your "steering" feel second nature.

* * * *

COMMON QUESTIONS

"That's it? That's the Fast Practice Formula?"

Yeah, that's right.

Don't let the simplicity of the Fast Practice Formula fool you.

the Fast Practice Formula is the secret sauce to over 20,000 of my guitar students all over the world playing the songs they love on guitar.

I'm not only the creator of the Fast Practice Formula, I use it myself to navigate my Fast Practice Sessions.

Every time I practice!

And it's taken me 22 years to get my practice technique to this level of simplicity.

* * * *

"Why play the Chunk 3xWMM before moving on? Why not once or twice?"

If you play a Chunk once, you may have just gotten lucky.

If you play a Chunk twice in a row, it might still actually be luck.

In my playing & coaching experience, I've noticed that if you're able to play a Chunk three times in a row without making a mistake, it shows you really know how to play it.

You can't move on and expect to make rapid progress until you can play a Chunk 3xWMM.

* * * *

"What if the Chunk isn't the problem? What if it's something else?"

Even though modifying the Chunk's speed, length, and level of complexity is the best way to play a part 3xWMM...

There may be times when your mind fully understands what your fingers are supposed to play, but your fingers just don't cooperate.

In these rare situations, it's likely that either:

- your guitar angle (up or down), or your guitar tilt (towards you or away from you) needs to be adjusted...
- The part of your fingertip/fingerprint you're using to press the string or your wrist position (rotation and bend) needs to be modified...
- you need to hold more of the pick to increase your accuracy...
- you need to use a lighter pick for less friction or a heavier pick for more control...
- you are too hunched over or leaning too far back and you just need to sit upright...

OR

- you have way too much on your mind and you aren't following the Fast Practice Formula.

Stop.

Take a deep breath.

Now zoom out and think of a few potential obstacles from the list above that are preventing you from playing the Chunk (i.e. if your guitar is pointing to the floor and tilted back to you, and you're hunched over with your fingers looking like a contorted monster claw).

Adjust one of the elements and try the Chunk again.

Troubleshoot for a couple of minutes to find an adjustment that works.

Go back to playing the Chunk so slow you can't make a mistake (Slow Tempo Practice) if you have to.

And if all else fails, reach out to me (**support@rockstarmind.com**) or another guitar expert for help, so you can get back on track with playing the Chunk in question 3xWMM.

* * * *

"Why modify the Speed by only 3-5bpm?"

I get asked this question a lot.

When I used to build up the speed of riffs I used to learn, I would add 1bpm each time.

The logic being that an increase in speed of 1bpm would trick my mind into thinking I was playing the same tempo the entire time as I inched up to the target tempo.

This is because every 1bpm increment felt exactly the same as the previous tempo, so my Stress Meter wouldn't shoot up as I increased the speed.

It was a great hack, but it took way too long to get to the target tempo.

I've found that 3-5bpm gives you a similar effect and saves you a ton of time.

5bpm is the absolute max interval to increase before your mind starts to notice the speed difference and wreak havoc.

3bpm is the sweet spot.

* * * *

"What if my timer sounds the alarm before I complete my Top Priority Task (TPT)?"

It's very likely that at first, your timer will go off before you complete your TPT.

Especially when you're only practicing 5 or 10 minutes per day.

Your TPT is probably too ambitious or the Chunk you chose is probably too complex.

You're still getting used to the PRACTICE LESS, PLAY MORE! system and eventually you'll set new TPTs and create new Chunks that are more suitable for the amount of time you have to practice...

Practice Time: 10 minutes

Decent TPT: Play "Wish You Were Here"

Good TPT: Learn the Intro to "Wish You Were Here"

Great TPT: Learn the first Intro lick of "Wish You Were Here" up to the first G chord (at full speed)

If you can't complete your TPT by the end of today's Fast Practice Session, then start tomorrow's Fast Practice Session by practicing the same Chunk you left off with today using No Tempo Practice.

And begin the process all over again...

No Tempo Practice -> Slow Tempo Practice -> Fast Practice Formula

Take as many Fast Practice Sessions as you need to iron out each Chunk until you can play them 3xWMM.

Remember, the first Phases in this book are more about programming a reliable practice habit and internalizing the practice techniques laid out in the book, so try not to put too much pressure on yourself to get things perfect right away.

Any time you learn a new system, you're learning both the skill AND the steps to learn that skill at the same time.

Once you get used to the steps, you can focus 100% of your energy on the skill.

words, your Fast Practice Sessions will only get faster and you keep using them.

"When is the best time for me to practice?"

While there is no universal practice time that will work for everyone, I have found that the best time for the brain to process, store, and organize new information is as close to bedtime as possible.

Without getting too science-y here, the closer you can get your Fast Practice Sessions to the time you fall asleep, the better your brain can organize the information and commit it to long term memory.

(This is assuming you'll have a good night's sleep of at least 6-8 hours of deep Delta sleep where your subconscious mind can do its thing)

It's kind of like having your own personal assistant filing your important data into a filing cabinet while you are dreaming of rocking Madison Square Garden.

It's why the Pillow Trick from Chapter 4 is so effective…

…and one of the main reasons I schedule #PajamaJAMs to be right before I go to sleep.

I've lost count of how many times I've struggled with a guitar part during my "pre-sleep practice session" and then almost magically, the next day, it would be completely sorted out.

INSERT APPLAUSE

"For my next trick I'd like to…"

It doesn't mean there's little to no benefit to practicing at any other time of day…

This is just one more practice accelerator to add to your toolbox, so you can Practice Less, and PLAY More!

It's definitely one of my favourite practice hacks that you should try out if you aren't already practicing at night.

* * * *

"What section of the song should I start learning? Should I always start from the beginning of the song?"

The section of the song you start learning is determined by what you want to get out of the song.

If you only want to play the signature riff of "Beat It" then start there and move onto another song/riff once you can play it.

If you're developing your fingerpicking technique and you love the pattern in "Landslide" then start at the beginning and consider learning the entire song.

If you're focused on soloing technique and "Comfortably Numb" contains your favourite guitar solos, then start with one solo and then learn the other.

The best part about music is that there are SO many songs to choose from and so many lessons contained in each one.

No one said you have to learn each one from front to back.

Like an all-u-can-eat buffet, it's also ok to sample pieces of songs.

I do it all the time.

Just ask yourself what it is you want to get out of the experience (i.e. having fun. developing a new technique, learning a song for a live ɛ, etc.) and start with the part that makes the most sense ɪt goal.

ESS, PLAY MORE!

And if you don't know where to start, then start at the beginning and see where the song takes you.

I have plenty of students who only want to learn the signature parts of songs and plenty of students who insist on learning the entire song.

Sometimes you might start learning a song only wanting to learn one part and because you have so much fun with it, you decide to learn the whole thing.

The choice of where to start and how much to play is 100% yours.

And as long as you're happy, I'm happy.

* * * *

"Will I be able to learn ANY song with the Fast Practice Formula?"

The short answer is yes, however it's important to be realistic with your expectations.

For example, you won't be able to rock all of Yngwie Malmsteen's Rising Force in one sitting if you just bought a guitar this afternoon.

Strum-along songs and Power Chords are more suited for you if that's the case.

Depending on your current level of playing, some songs will take longer than others because of the techniques and musculature required to execute them (i.e. faster songs, complex picking patterns, fingerpicking, etc.).

We can't escape the fact that there is a physical component to playing the guitar and sometimes, certain songs just take more time to play.

The good news is that the Fast Practice Formula will help you play any song in the shortest amount of time possible for YOU!

So if you're trying to play a more complex guitar part, you won't have to worry about running in circles for months without making any progress.

With the Fast Practice Formula, the song you're learning will take you a concrete amount of time to play (i.e. 6 weeks) and you'll always know that each time you practice you will be making steady progress towards your goal.

Even though you won't know exactly how long it will take for you to play the song, you will know that by following the steps in this chapter, you'll be able to play the song effortlessly in the shortest amount of time possible.

* * * *

Now that you know the Fast Practice Formula…

Let's dive right into a real Fast Practice Session, so you can see all 3 steps - No Tempo Practice, Slow Tempo Practice, and the Fast Practice Formula - in action.

LET'S PRACTICE!

Alright! You have the right mindset dialled in, you have your Pre-Practice material ready to go, and you played a little bit of guitar to grease the wheels.

Now it's time to actually practice!

I know the explanations might seem long, consisting of so many components for you to add to your practice session, however when you actually go through a real Fast Practice Session as we're about to do, you'll see it is a very simple & natural process.

The first thing you will do is look at the practice material you gathered in Pre-Practice earlier today.

Let's say you found a lyric & chord sheet for Free Fallin' by Tom Petty and the Heartbreakers.

Set your timer for the appropriate amount of practice time (see Chapter 4 for details).

You have 10 minutes to practice and your Top Priority Task for today is to play the Intro of Free Fallin' up to speed with the record.

In Pre-Practice, you noticed that the Intro chords are all chords you know how to play - D, G, and Asus4, so you didn't see any red flags when you quickly scanned through the lyric sheet.

You also noticed that the tempo of Free Fallin' is 84bpm and it needs a capo on Fret 3, so you prepared a capo and a metronome set to 84bpm earlier.

Put the capo on Fret 3, and start your 10-minute timer.

FREE FALLIN' - NO TEMPO PRACTICE

Begin to play through the 5-chord sequence in the Intro - D G G D Asus4 - with no concern for speed or a steady pulse.

Strum one Downstroke on each new chord.

Go at a pace that allows you to think clearly and maintain control the entire time.

Mark down any areas of the Intro (if any) that might be a potential problem area.

FREE FALLIN' - SLOW TEMPO PRACTICE

Now that you scanned through the entire Intro with No Tempo Practice, you're ready to play the 5-chord sequence - D G G D Asus4 -one time with a steady tempo using Slow Tempo Practice...

This is your first Chunk...

And you set your metronome to 55bpm because this is the tempo that feels so slow you can't make a mistake.

You play the first Chunk successfully and are now ready to use the Fast Practice Formula to solidify the Chunk.

FREE FALLIN' - FAST PRACTICE FORMULA

You attempt to play the Chunk a second time.

You play it successfully again.

That's two times without making a mistake.

You're close to solidifying the Chunk and moving on.

You attempt the Chunk for the third time, but you get too excited and your pick slips, causing you to make a mistake.

This resets your counter back to zero.

You realize you were hunching over your guitar too much, so you adjust and try again.

You play the Chunk three times without making a mistake (with a pause in between each attempt).

Congratulations! You just completed your first Chunk at 3xWMM.

You "move on" by increasing the speed by 5bpm from 55bpm to 60bpm.

You play the same Chunk 3xWMM.

You move on by increasing the speed by 5bpm to 65bpm.

This continues until you get to 80bpm, which is only 4bpm from the target tempo.

You move on by increasing the amount to double the size of the Chunk (creating one MEGA Chunk) and playing the 5-chord sequence - D G G D Asus4 - twice, which is the full Intro of Free Fallin'.

You play this Chunk 3xWMM and you're feeling confident, so you decide you want to try to play along with the record (a great strategy by the way).

You get distracted by trying to match the chords and you make two mistakes in a row (2MR).

You "go back" by playing the same Chunk at 80bpm without the record.

You play the Chunk 3xWMM.

You move on by playing with the record again and this time you play 3xWMM.

Top Priority Task accomplished!

Your timer expires and the alarm goes off.

Congratulations! You just completed your first Fast Practice Session.

Tomorrow you can warm up with this section when you PLAY before your Fast Practice Session begins.

* * * *

Pretty cool, right?

This is just one example of a Fast Practice Session.

Check out the "PRACTICE LESS, PLAY MORE!" Book Resources page online for more examples of a Fast Practice Session and be sure to try one out for yourself today.

The best way to learn the steps is to experience them for yourself.

My students find this method of practicing to be way more fun & enjoyable than the conventional method of practicing where you just practice the same part over and over and hope for the best.

They say Fast Practice Sessions feel like playing a game where you're trying to get a score of 3 before moving on to the next level…

…and I couldn't agree more!

TROUBLESHOOTING YOUR FAST PRACTICE SESSION

Before wrapping up this section, I wanted to include a few troubleshooting tips in case things aren't going according to plan.

The Fast Practice Formula is all about navigation, so I want to make sure you always know what to do, whether your playing is going well or your playing has gone to Hell. ;)

One of the most common things you'll encounter is that you automatically revert back to whatever style of practicing you used to use...

...instead of following the Fast Practice Formula.

This is usually triggered by making a mistake while attempting to play a Chunk.

Instead of thinking about 2MR or going back to something less difficult to play...

Your natural tendency will be to stop right away, frantically start from the beginning, and maybe even play the Chunk a bit faster (almost as if you're trying to make up for lost time).

Don't worry.

I still fight with this same tendency from time to time and it's something I have to constantly remember to keep in check.

This is your inner Perfectionist trying to hijack your practice session, so you want to catch yourself whenever possible and use the Fast Practice Formula to get back on track.

The same goes for when things are going well.

When you're able to play a Chunk 3xWMM, it might tempt you to just jump right into playing the song at full speed.

Taking the cake out of the oven WAY before it's ready.

I still fight this tendency too because it's hard not to be excited when you play something 3xWMM.

No problem.

Just catch yourself when you do this and instead of playing the end result right away, use one of the 3 Modifiers to increase the Speed, Amount, or Complexity of the current Chunk...

...and then keep working the steps from there.

When you're able to play the guitar parts up to speed using the Fast Practice Formula, you will have a much more solid & reliable end-product and you can actually enjoy the experience of playing the song on guitar...

...instead of trying to hold on for dear life to keep up with the tempo.

* * * *

My final tip for this section is to write down any obstacles or questions you might have for a coach, a friend who plays guitar, or a guitar expert, while they are still fresh in your mind.

You will likely forget these questions, so make sure to jot them down as they come up in your Fast Practice Session.

The bonus of jotting these down is that you will have a list of potential TPTs to tackle as well as other material you'll need to Hunt & Gather for tomorrow's Pre-Practice.

AND IT NEEDS TO GO ON AND ON AND ON AND ON

The Fast Practice Formula is so powerful because it removes the element of failure from your practice sessions.

It's like you're a scientist stepping into your laboratory (your practice space) and conducting experiments (your Chunks).

If the Chunk you start with is too easy to play, you'll know because you'll be able to play it 3xWMM and then you'll move on to practicing something more difficult.

If the Chunk you start with is too difficult to play, you'll know right away because you'll make 2 mistakes in a row and then you'll go back to practicing something less difficult.

And the process keeps going like that until you can achieve your Top Priority Task and ultimately, your 90-day goal.

The Fast Practice Formula makes your Practice sessions extremely productive and efficient, so you can achieve a lot even if you only have 5 or 10 minutes to practice per day.

REMINDER

If you feel stuck at ANY point, whether it's knowing how to start with a basic Chunk or knowing how to work with one of the 3 Modifiers (Speed, Amount, Complexity), please reach out to me at **support@rockstarmind.com** and I will help you get unstuck.

After experiencing a few Fast Practice Sessions for yourself, the steps will just get easier and easier for you…

…to the point where creating the right Chunk at the right time and modifying it with the Fast Practice Formula becomes second nature.

ACTION ITEMS TO INCREASE YOUR SONG PLAYLIST

1. Start your practice timer and scan through today's TPT with No Tempo Practice.
2. Select your first Chunk and practice it with Slow Tempo Practice.
3. Use the Fast Practice Formula to tackle your TPT until the timer goes off.

* * * *

MORE READING/LISTENING

Visit **PracticeLessPlayMore.com** for a secret bonus chapter plus a list of recommended resources and additional notes that expand on this topic.

Chapter 8:
Play AFTER You Practice

If you've made it to this step, it means you've completed your first Fast Practice Session.

Congratulations again!

Remember, it isn't about perfection at this point (or really ever).

It's about adopting an efficient practice method like the PRACTICE LESS, PLAY MORE! system that gets you the fastest results possible, even if you only have 5-10 minutes to practice per day.

As I mentioned before, any great system...

Saves
You
Stress
Time
Energy and
Money

So continue to work the system and you will experience more benefits each time you use it.

At this point…

- You've completed your Pre-Practice…
- You've started your Fast Practice Session by playing something that feels effortless…

AND

- You've completed your first Fast Practice Session.

Amazing!

Now it's time to finish with more effortless playing.

It's so important that you play something that feels easy for you AFTER your Fast Practice Session.

You must always keep effortless playing and having fun at the forefront and that's why you will sandwich your Fast Practice Session with more Playing.

Even if it's for only 30 seconds or a minute.

Once your timer expires for your Fast Practice Session and the alarm goes off, it's time to PLAY the song you were just working on in the session.

This is where you get the payoff for the work you just put in.

And it also reminds you that you should always be playing MUSIC.

To make sure this doesn't turn into another Fast Practice Session, you will play along with the original record *(at any speed that's comfortable for you)*.

There are a lot of easy-to-use software and apps that help you tweak the speed and key of your favourite records.

(I will share my recommended software & apps list in the Bonus Chapter, which you can find on the PRACTICE LESS, PLAY MORE! Book Resources page online)

For now, we will use YouTube because it's the easiest option, it's FREE, and it comes with a decent speed control function.

It doesn't matter what speed you play the record.

What matters is you are playing along.

And you'll accomplish that by imagining you're standing on stage with the band.

THE STANDING ON STAGE (S.O.S.) METHOD

Many guitarists I have coached told me they felt intimidated when it comes to playing along with a record.

Almost as if they aren't ready and aren't worthy to play along.

This is usually their inner Perfectionist talking (as I described in Chapter 2).

No problem at all.

It's nothing a couple of days of playing along with your favourite records won't fix. ;)

If you're currently feeling the same way, then I assure you, you ARE ready and you're DEFINITELY worthy to play along with the record.

In fact, playing along with your favourite records is going to be a major part of your development on the guitar.

The reason most guitarists feel so intimidated when it comes to playing along is because they feel like they need to play every single detail they hear on the record...

Up to speed...

Just like their guitar heroes on the records do...

Have you ever felt like that?

The good news is that's the exact problem S.O.S. fixes.

Basically, S.O.S. (Standing On Stage) is all about imagining yourself standing on stage with the band.

What that means is you are showing up to THEIR performance and are letting THEM take the spotlight.

All the pressure is on THEM and THEY are doing all the heavy lifting.

You're just an additional member of the band.

And all you have to do is follow along with literally any guitar part that is compatible with what they're playing.

It could be playing along with Single Strums...

Playing Power Chords instead of Open Chords...

Or even muffling the strings with your fretting hand and strumming Downstrokes to the pulse of the song...

Whatever is easiest for you.

This approach is extremely helpful for you as a guitarist, no matter what level of playing you're currently at.

Because you get to have all the fun, without being intimidated by having to play the exact part on the record perfectly and up to speed.

Instead of playing their exact parts, you play whatever suits your current skill level.

Pretty cool, right?

The purpose of Playing after your Fast Practice Session is to remind yourself of these 3 important things:

1) The guitar is meant to play music…
2) Playing guitar should feel effortless…
3) Playing guitar is supposed to be fun!

So with those in mind, you have my blessing to crank up the volume, play like a kid, and enjoy yourself.

This switch from Practice Mode to Playing Mode after your session is a crucial one, so even though I want you to have fun, I also want you to take playing along seriously and never skip this step.

We'll call it Serious Fun.

Deal?

A QUICK NOTE IF PLAYING ALONG ISN'T FEELING EFFORTLESS

Even though you can almost always find a guitar part to play along with the record…

If playing along with the record is too difficult for you and you can't figure out how to gel with the other instruments, then it's ok.

I recommend cranking the record and playing along anyway.

I can't emphasize enough how important it is that playing along becomes a regular part of your routine.

Sometimes practicing can feel like you're in a bubble and you are so focused on what you're trying to play that you don't even notice anything that's going on around you.

I see this all the time with Beginner Guitarists.

One of the main benefits of playing along with records (especially if you're playing something simple) is that it raises your awareness that there are other musicians and moving parts that exist outside of the bubble…

…and your job is to gel with them.

This awareness is what helps you develop your musical toolbox like timing, tone, and intonation.

It also frees you up to concentrate on your vocals if you plan to sing songs while you play guitar.

Truthfully, you don't have to think about any of that stuff right now while you play.

I just wanted you to know about it, so you know you're getting the benefits as a natural side effect of playing along with records regularly.

If you don't have an easy way to play a record after your Fast Practice

Session (i.e. on your computer, on your phone with headphones, etc.)

Then you can either play the simplest version of the song you just worked on in your Fast Practice Session...

...or you can play something else that feels effortless.

A couple of chords...

An easy riff...

Something simple.

As a fail-safe, you can even play the same exact thing that you played before your Fast Practice Session started.

Playing along with the recorded version of the song you just worked on in your Fast Practice Session is ideal...

...however, if you can't make it happen today, then playing anything will be better than nothing since it still puts the emphasis on playing music.

HOW LONG SHOULD YOU PLAY AFTER YOUR FAST PRACTICE SESSION?

Since this final Playing step is extremely important for your mind and your confidence, we don't want to skip it.

Why skip something that's fun?

By playing along with the record after your Fast Practice Session you are telling yourself that playing music is the most important element of being a guitarist.

Because that's the step you're ending with.

Our minds are great at remembering the ending.

And just like before, Playing after your session will take about 10% of your practice time.

So that works out to 30 seconds of additional time for a 5-minute Fast Practice Session and one minute if your Fast Practice Session is 10 minutes long.

Once again, always make sure to play before and after your practice sessions.

Even if the 10% before and 10% after eat into your actual practice time.

It's that important.

Before we wrap up this chapter, I want to share one more tool with you that I highly recommend you use after you finish playing for the day.

THE PROGRESS BOOSTER

The Progress Booster is a simple tool that helps you stay on top of your overall practice habit.

It consists of two components:

1) Starting/Continuing your Winning Streak (see Chapter 4 for details)

and 2) Setting your Top Priority Task for tomorrow's Fast Practice Session

Now that your Fast Practice Session is complete and you are finished playing guitar for the day, you can mark an X on your calendar or dedicated streak app to start/continue your Winning Streak.

It will be cool to see the chain get longer and longer as you complete more Fast Practice Sessions.

Next, I recommend setting your Top Priority Task (TPT) for tomorrow based on what went well today and what still needs work.

The added benefit of setting your TPT today is that you can save yourself time tomorrow when you Pre-Practice.

You will begin Pre-Practice and you'll already know the most relevant thing you need to accomplish today…

…so you can get right into Hunting & Gathering and preparing other materials for your Fast Practice Session.

The Progress Booster only takes about 30 seconds to complete and it will be well worth it for how much control and momentum it gives you.

* * * *

That just about wraps up the core of the PRACTICE LESS, PLAY MORE! system.

Next, we'll quickly discuss some other useful techniques you can add to your Fast Practice Session once it becomes a comfortable process for you.

While these techniques aren't mandatory, adding them will cut your learning time and help you on your path to Practice Less and PLAY More!

ACTION ITEMS TO INCREASE YOUR SONG PLAYLIST

1. Load up the record on YouTube for the song you're learning and set it to either 0.5, 0.75, or Normal speed *(whatever is easiest for you)*.
2. Start a timer that's 10% of the duration of your Fast Practice Session.
3. Play along with the record until the alarm goes off.

---

* * * *

MORE READING/LISTENING

Visit **PracticeLessPlayMore.com** for a secret bonus chapter plus a list of recommended resources and additional notes that expand on this topic.

Chapter 9:
Other Useful Mindsets &
Techniques

Even though you now have everything you need to improve your guitar technique and play the songs you love…

…like a G.P.S. (Guitar Practice System) helping you navigate the rest of your journey on guitar…

I wanted to include some helpful extras that you can add on to your Fast Practice Sessions to really enhance them and further shorten your practice time.

The list below includes useful mindsets and practical techniques you can use right away.

I recommend only adding a maximum of ONE of these per week so as not to overwhelm yourself by doing too much at once.

Let's begin with the mindsets…

W.I.N. - WHAT'S IMPORTANT NOW?

In *Essentialism: The Disciplined Pursuit of Less*, author Greg

McKeown writes about famous Notre Dame football coach Lou Holtz and his simple yet powerful acronym W.I.N., which stands for "What's Important Now?"

Holtz instructed his players to ask themselves this simple question 35 times a day - when they woke up, when they were in class, and DEFINITELY while they were on the football field.

Holtz wanted his players to be able to learn to focus on what mattered most at any given time by always bringing their attention back to "What's Important Now?"

It was one of the core mindsets for the team as they went to nine straight New Year's Day bowl games from 1987 through 1995 (winning 5 of 9) - a nearly unheard-of accomplishment.

What a great little acronym that fits perfectly with the PRACTICE LESS, PLAY MORE! philosophy.

Instead of getting discouraged by your mistakes or wasting mental energy getting distracted by all the potential things you could be practicing, neither of which is helpful or constructive while practicing your guitar…

…simply focus ONLY on what's important, which is the Chunk you're practicing right now and making sure you play it successfully 3xWMM.

And if you zoom out to your Top Priority Tasks and your 90-day goal, you can see the importance of making sure everything is aligned.

In order to guarantee you win each game you create, you must always stay focused on what's important now.

I call the next technique "Follow The Leader" and it is half mindset and half practical.

You'll see what I mean in a second…

FOLLOW THE LEADER & THE PLAYING PYRAMID

I've noticed that most Beginners & Struggling guitarists tend to look at the wrong hand or focus on the wrong things while practicing.

Instead, let's build on the W.I.N. technique above, where you ask yourself "What's important now?" and use the answer to better inform your decisions.

This will help you focus your eyes on where the main action is and help you focus your mind on where to direct its attention.

If you don't know how to direct your focus, what I find typically happens is…

- Guitarists will look exclusively at their fretting hand and let it lead the way no matter what their strumming hand has to play (i.e. they are currently strumming an A Major chord and they're about to switch to F# minor, but when they make the chord switch, their strumming hand completely stops and waits until the new chord is fully formed before strumming again)

AND/OR

- Guitarists will look exclusively at their strumming hand,

become obsessed about the exact strings they need to pick or strum (causing a lot of tension and a stop-and-go strumming effect) when they should really be focused on maintaining a steady pulse (aka "The Flow") and not worrying so much about hitting all the correct strings right away

AND/OR

- Guitarists will gaze off into the distance and not actually think about what's going on, leading to a tug of war between the strumming hand and fretting hand and a bunch of random mistakes

If that sounds like what you're doing, then let's fix this right away.

To correct this issue, we need structure.

We need a ranking system.

Sometimes it's tricky to know what's important now and you might need a more visual example to drive the concept home.

So that's where Follow The Leader & The Playing Pyramid come in.

I was recently helping one of my clients (John L. from Houston, Texas) play along with "Here Comes the Sun" by The Beatles.

He was building the chords pretty well…

But when he started to strum, his timing was WAY off and everything fell apart.

And I totally get it.

He said he couldn't get his hands to sync up…

Like his hands were playing a bad game of Follow The Leader.

So I told him we actually DO want to play Follow The Leader...

...only he just chose the wrong leader.

As I mentioned earlier, it's VERY common for guitarists to choose the wrong hand to lead the way.

So that's when I introduced John to "The Playing Pyramid".

As a general rule...

- Your fretting hand takes care of the WHAT (the notes & chords)...
- Your strumming hand takes care of the WHEN (the rhythm & groove)...

AND

- Your voice – yes, your voice – takes care of the COUNTING (the pulse)...

Your voice is the leader of your strumming hand...

And your strumming hand is the leader of your fretting hand.

So in other words...

Your chords & melodies have to follow your strumming & picking which all follow your voice.

That's the game of "Follow The Leader" we want to play.

I mean it makes sense, doesn't it?

You've been speaking much longer than you've been playing guitar, so you might as well use your voice to your advantage to maintain a steady musical pulse…

Since it's the easiest of the three to control…

Right?

And more often than not, your strumming will be your main focus, locking in with the steady pulse and steady count of your voice while your chords follow along no matter what.

Just by keeping that steady pulse going the entire time will instantly make you sound more Pro and less amateur.

Even if you're making some mistakes on the chord side…

…you can always slow things down or tweak your chord switching technique to make it to the next chord in time.

At least now it sounds like music because of the steady pulse.

IMPORTANT: If you are worried about your chords being a little sloppy, then it's time to say our mantra out loud: "Play now, polish later."

Back to our story…

So once John started counting out loud…

"1 2 3 4 1 2 3 4…etc."

And strumming each chord ONLY ONCE for one full four count (aka "Single Strumming")…

A Major, A Major, D Major, E Major

His strumming was perfectly in time because it was following his voice.

And his chord changes became effortless because he now had a specific target to hit (the next strum), so he knew exactly when he had to switch to the next chord.

So naturally, when John put the record on and played/counted along, he locked in perfectly with George Harrison and Co.

John said it felt like Target Practice.

All he had to do was count out loud to the pulse of the record and match up the chords…

He totally nailed it!

Safe to say, John was stoked.

To build on his success, I now asked John to play a Downstroke on every beat he counted out loud…

"1 2 3 4 1 2 3 4…etc."

And strum each chord on EVERY BEAT (aka "Steady Strumming")…

Same chords…different strumming…same focus on the pulse.

"A 2 3 4, A 2 3 4, D 2 3 4, E 2 3 4"

And just like before, John locked in with the record.

Amazing!

These wins gave him something solid to work with before he tackled the more complex Strumming & Picking Pattern that's heard on the record.

Pretty cool, right?

The moral of the story is when coordinating your Chord Switches & Strumming Patterns, make sure to give yourself an unfair advantage by playing a game of Follow The Leader where the chords follow the strumming and the strumming follows the voice (aka "The Playing Pyramid").

Sometimes your voice might say the Strumming Pattern out loud (i.e. "Down DownUp UpDownUp") instead of the counting ("1 2 3 4 1 2 3 4"), but the same concept applies.

THE POWER OF CONTRAST

The Power Of Contrast is a simple technique that can produce massive results in your guitar playing.

More like a mind hack and something you definitely want to incorporate after you have a few songs under your belt...

The Power Of Contrast is when you purposely tackle a song or guitar part that you know is going to be too advanced for you to play.

The idea is to really marinate in the complexity for one or two practice sessions and don't try to simplify any parts.

Like Chinese water torture for guitar, but you asked for it.

You will get frustrated, but you knew that.

You will get overwhelmed, but you expected that.

You might hate the song you're playing for a little while, and that's totally fine, you had a feeling that might happen.

Now go back to a song you were practicing before this or start a new riff that's more in your realm of skill level and voila!

Everything will feel WAY easier to play.

Almost like taking a vacation.

You can accomplish the same thing with equipment (discussed in Chapter 10) where you purposely put heavier gauge strings on your guitar, struggle with it for a couple of days, and then return to your original gauge (or lighter) to reap the benefits.

A mini version of The Power Of Contrast is when you're getting close to playing a song up to speed and are having a hard time getting all the way to 100% speed.

Once you get to 90% or 95% of the target tempo, you can skip to 105%, 110%, or even 120% of the target tempo…

Try to keep up for 5 minutes…

…and then go down to the target speed of 100% where it will feel slow by comparison.

What once seemed gruelling, like trying to climb up a mountain, now feels like going down a slide.

The Power Of Contrast is one of my favourite Practice Power Tools, so I hope you enjoy it.

WARNING: The Power Of Contrast is only for Guitar Players who have a solid practice habit and have been using the PRACTICE LESS, PLAY MORE! system for over a month. It will only distract and discourage you if you use this advanced technique too early in the game.

PUZZLE PIECING

The next technique is more practical, and it is most useful when you have two or more Chunks developed.

And the best way to explain it is with an example.

Let's say, you are halfway through your Fast Practice Session and you can already play the first bar and second bar of "Sweet Home Alabama" up to speed - the D Major pattern (Chunk #1) and the Cadd9 pattern (Chunk #2), but you always make a mistake when you try connecting the Chunks.

Instead of rushing into playing both parts up to speed and fully connected…

Sometimes you'll have an easier time getting the part connected if you think of the two Chunks as puzzle pieces that you are gradually bringing closer together.

Since you can play each individual Chunk up to speed with the metronome (98bpm), we keep the metronome going and gradually close the gap to connect the Chunks (puzzle pieces) like this:

- Play Chunk #1, wait 4 clicks on your metronome, and then play Chunk #2 - play 3xWMM with pauses in between each attempt
- Play Chunk #1, wait 3 clicks on your metronome, and then play Chunk #2 - play 3xWMM with pauses in between each attempt
- Play Chunk #1, wait 2 clicks on your metronome, and then play Chunk #2 - play 3xWMM with pauses in between each attempt

Almost there…

We're closing the gap.

- Play Chunk #1, wait 1 click on your metronome, and then play Chunk #2 - play 3xWMM with pauses in between each attempt

And for the final connection…

- Play Chunk #1 right into Chunk #2 - play 3xWMM with pauses in between each attempt

That's how you puzzle-piece.

You can continue this if you like.

Chunk #1 and Chunk #2 can now become one MEGA Chunk and you can eventually connect it to other Chunks in the same way.

This is a super powerful technique!

THE MIRROR

The final technique I'll show you is actually one that I want you to incorporate ASAP.

Since practicing and playing guitar require so much of your brain's resources, there's really no way for you to fully keep track of everything you're doing including...

- Catching bad habits like slouching, hunching over, or bending your wrist of your fretting hand at a 90-degree angle

OR

- Noticing that every time you make a mistake, you stop right away and play the next attempt faster and from the beginning as if trying to make up for lost time

OR

- Spotting the things you're doing well and making sure you keep doing them in order to progress faster on guitar.

There are so many more obvious & subtle things that I can list here, ˙ ˙ ˙ ˙ ˙ ˙ ˙ you get how we need all the help we can get...

Especially since you also have to take care of learning chord shapes & Strumming Patterns…

…up to speed…

…with the record.

So in order to focus your Fast Practice Sessions on what's important now and spot any bad habits & tendencies that can prevent you from playing the songs you love…

We're going to need help.

I call this help "The Mirror."

I've tried being too literal with this concept in the past by practicing in front of an actual mirror…

…but that caused me to make too many mistakes because my focus was on looking at the mirror the whole time instead of my guitar and I had to make sense of the backwards reflection.

Safe to say, it was taxing on my brain.

It was a good idea in theory, but not in practice.

So instead, we're going to use a more figurative mirror.

And we turn to video.

You will record a video of yourself playing using whatever device is easiest for you to use…

- a smartphone
- a webcam

OR

- a Panasonic OmniMovie camcorder from the 80s

Just make sure the room is lit fairly well, is pretty quiet, and your fretting hand and strumming hand are both in the frame.

The reason I call this technique "The Mirror" is because I compare practicing guitar WITHOUT recording yourself to shaving without a mirror.

I don't know about you, but shaving without a mirror or in the dark would be an absolute disaster.

You can miss a spot (or ten), it takes longer to finish, and you can get seriously hurt.

When you record your Fast Practice Sessions, you get to wear your Guitarist Cap when you're practicing & playing…

And then you get to wear your Coach's Cap when you watch the video.

This is how you might discover that every time you're about to switch chords, you look far off into the distance instead of looking at the chord to ensure a good switch.

This is how you might see your head bouncing back and forth between fretting hand and strumming hand like a bobble head.

Or you might see how tapping your foot on the floor is actually throwing off the timing of your solo.

You do those things without even realizing it and the only way to catch them (along with any other habits or tendencies that might hold you back) is to record them and then watch the recording.

You can record your video, review it in your spare time or during Pre-Practice, take any notes to remember for your next practice session, and then delete it.

However, I HIGHLY recommend you keep every video.

Your videos will also act as a great progress monitor where you can document your first attempt at a song and then track your progress throughout its development.

When you achieve certain milestones like being able to play a song you love up to speed with the record and you document it on video, that will act as a huge motivator for you and will be a great pick-me-up if you ever have a bad day where you question your ability to play guitar.

All of my online coaching programs involve students posting their videos either to me or to a private group for feedback and to celebrate their successes.

It might be a little awkward to record yourself at first, but soon it will become a necessary part of your Fast Practice Routine.

You'll find that you always play a little worse when the recording light (aka "The Red-Light Monster") is on, but I promise you'll get better at it and you'll always know that you played so much better when you weren't recording, so it's ok.

* * * *

I hope you can incorporate some of these powerful techniques into your Fast Practice Sessions.

They have worked wonders in my own guitar playing and have helped over 20,000 of my guitar students around the world play an average of 2-3 songs per week on their guitar.

Always remember to introduce each technique gradually and then feel free to use them as you need them.

CONCLUSION TO PART 2

Wow. You made it!

That concludes the PRACTICE portion of the book.

You've learned some killer practice techniques that I wish I had when I was first learning how to play guitar.

For the rest of the book, I will cover everything that goes into PLAYING guitar effortlessly and provide you with more examples & resources to play the songs you love.

ACTION ITEMS TO INCREASE YOUR SONG PLAYLIST

1. Pick one of the mindsets or techniques above and incorporate it into your next Fast Practice Session.
2. Record a video of tomorrow's Fast Practice Session using something simple like your smartphone or webcam.
3. Watch your video and take note of 3 things you are doing well and 3 things you can improve on in your next Fast Practice Session.

* * * *

MORE READING/LISTENING

Visit **PracticeLessPlayMore.com** for a secret bonus chapter plus a list of recommended resources and additional notes that expand on this topic.

STOP!

If you are planning on actually using this method to play the songs you love on the guitar, stop reading right now, and go pick up your guitar.

The rest of the book is irrelevant and useless until you can actually play a song *(or part of a song)* that you are happy with.

Seriously. STOP READING.

Go work the steps and begin your first Fast Practice Session now.

PART 3: PLAY

Chapter 10:
Now That You Can Play A Song

Congratulations!

If you've made it this far, then it means that you can play a song (or part of a song) effortlessly, which is more than A LOT of Beginners and struggling guitarists can say.

That's amazing and I am so proud of you!

Hopefully, you're having fun with the PRACTICE LESS, PLAY MORE! system so far.

I'm having a blast walking you through it.

This is really just the beginning for you.

As long as you do the work and incorporate the techniques laid out in the previous two sections, it's only a matter of time before you become a human jukebox with the ability to play dozens of songs on your guitar.

After about 7-10 days, you will start to have a list of things you can play effortlessly.

Maybe it's a simple version of a song you love…

A simple riff like "You Really Got Me" by The Kinks...

Or even a simple solo like "Smells Like Teen Spirit" by Nirvana.

After about 30-45 days you'll have a long list of songs and parts of songs that you can play, which means you will have a lot of options of what to play when you pick up your guitar...

...because you will now have a Song Playlist.

This chapter will discuss how you can make the most of your growing Song Playlist including:

- Your ideal Mindset while playing guitar...
- What to play and when to play it...
- How to deal with mistakes (this one is HUGE)...
- How to keep your Song Playlist organized...

AND

- How to stay on top of your equipment

YOUR IDEAL MINDSET WHILE PLAYING GUITAR

The hard work is over.

The thinking part is done.

And if you tend to over-think things like I do, then you'll be happy to know that Playing Guitar is all about having a clear mind and just enjoying the peaceful, easy feeling.

As if you're a member of the audience listening in.

That's why it feels so good to just let loose and play songs you love on your guitar.

It's like an escape from reality and a cathartic release…

…a time machine to take you back to hearing "Appetite For Destruction" for the first time…

Or a way to travel deep through some black hole into some kind of vortex deep within.

(OK, maybe a little too psychedelic there, Steve)

You get my point.

In Practice Mode, your mind is required to do many things…

- Decide what the Top Priority Task is for each of your Fast Practice Sessions…
- Find high-quality TABs, chord diagrams, and videos for the songs you want to learn…
- Transfer the information you see in each TAB, chord diagram, or video to your fingers…

AND

- Steer the car with the Fast Practice Formula, so you can monitor your progress, simplify guitar parts on the fly, and execute them 3xWMM

To name a few.

Once the guitar parts are programmed into your fingers and are out of your mind, your mind's job is completed.

You really don't need to rely on your mind that much anymore.

Maybe it will switch on once in a while as you're playing in order to remember if there's another Verse after Chorus 2 in the song…

Or concentrate for a couple of bars in order to nail a tricky lick.

Other than that, your mind should really take a backseat when you're in Playing Mode.

In fact, too much thinking while you're playing can actually lead to mistakes.

So that's why it's important you use the Fast Practice Formula and other tools I laid out in the book to practice, so you can thoroughly program the parts into your fingers, trust the work you've done, and let your muscle memory take over.

RELAXED ILLUSIONS

Playing songs on guitar should feel relaxed and effortless.

If you watch a video of any accomplished Guitar Player playing, you can usually block out their guitar with your hand and if you watch their face, it will look like they're just hanging out…

…as calmly as one would when waiting for a bus…

…and definitely NOT like they're playing an awesome tune on guitar!

Try it out.

Load up a video of one of your favourite Guitar Players playing a song, riff, or solo (preferably sitting down).

Now cover their guitar on the screen with one hand and notice how relaxed they look...

...as if they're just sitting there without any tension whatsoever.

(unless they are making ugly guitar faces or really "performing" the song on stage, but that's something entirely different)

When you're playing songs, you want your mind and your muscles to feel as relaxed as possible.

That mainly comes from having a solid understanding of all the guitar parts involved in the song, so your mind can unwind and your fingers can play the parts you programmed them to play in your Fast Practice Session.

The better your mind understands what to play, the better your fingers can execute each part in time with the record.

And if your mind wanders, it's ok.

Just bring your focus back to LISTENING to the music you're playing and your mind should stay out of the way for a bit.

This is why it's so important for you to play along with records (and other musicians) because the music that's happening outside of you will usually keep your mind occupied.

We'll touch on this topic some more in the following section.

If you catch yourself making a bunch of mistakes and it's affecting your enjoyment or your ability to play effortlessly, you'll want to bring the song back to the laboratory and work out any kinks in your next Fast Practice Session.

WHAT TO PLAY AND WHEN TO PLAY IT

You've heard me say it so many times by now:

"Play the songs you love."

"Play along with the original records."

I've said it to the point where it might even sound obvious.

But I can't stress the importance enough.

Playing along with your favourite records is so important in both your practice sessions and your playing sessions.

It will not only give you a solid base to play on top of to quickly make progress, but it will also develop the "micro-skills" you need to become a proficient musician.

Micro-skills are the skills that aren't as obvious like:

- Playing in time with the band...
- Playing in tune with the other instruments...
- Following the drummer for cues of what parts are coming up next...
- Waiting for other instruments to play their part first before entering with your guitar part (i.e. Intro or Re-Intro of a song)...
- Playing at the right volume so you blend in with the other instruments...

AND

- Not stopping after making a mistake on your guitar.

These are just a few of the micro-skills you'll develop when you make playing along with your favourite records a priority.

I think you'd also agree it's WAY more fun to play along with a record you love than it is to just play the song by yourself without any accompaniment.

PLAYING WITH PURPOSE

I mentioned this earlier in the book, but I'll mention it again because you are now a different Guitar Player after going through the PRACTICE LESS, PLAY MORE! system.

What you plan to accomplish may have changed and it will continue to change as you can play more & more songs on guitar.

When it comes to deciding what to play on guitar…

Dream big! Make it count! Always play with purpose!

Here are some ideas from my students' accomplishments that you can start with:

- Play a song for someone you love on a special occasion (or even surprise them with a song on a regular day)
- Jam with some buddies once a week
- Start a band and play your favourite tunes together
- Perform at an Open Mic
- Play along with your favourite album from when you were 16, in its entirety
- Go watch a concert and then come home to play along with the best songs of the night
- Explore different styles of music from around the world

(while traveling or while home) and start to learn songs from those genres

Let yourself be inspired and let that inspiration fuel your upcoming Practice & Playing sessions.

If you're ever playing or practicing something that doesn't align with one of your goals, then scrap it.

Your time is way too valuable to do anything that isn't serving your purpose.

And if you can't imagine doing any of the things I mentioned above…

No problem.

Your goals will change as your Song Playlist grows since it will boost your confidence and change what you believe is possible.

So something you could never imagine yourself doing before, like performing "Pink Houses" at an Open Mic or starting a Blues cover band with the guys from work…

…are now goals you can't wait to accomplish.

Remember, anything is possible when you keep an open mind and you do the work.

WHEN TO PLAY SONGS

Since you're probably picking up your guitar a lot more often these days and experiencing more musical results…

…it's important you split your time in a way that includes as much guitar playing as possible.

You already got a taste of this when you switched to "Playing Mode" right before your Fast Practice Session started and right after it ended.

Once you have songs on your Playlist, you will need to set aside some time that is strictly for PLAYING.

That's what the goal was when you wanted to learn how to play guitar, right?

To just pick up the guitar at any point of the day and just play a song.

- Unwinding after a long day at work…
- Impressing your friends at a party…

OR

- Playing a song for your kids or grandkids to sing along with.

These are the things we usually imagine…

…not sitting in a Fast Practice Session and working on parts.

Even though that IS very satisfying and fun to work out guitar parts when you have a structured system like I've been showing you.

I just mean, we dream of being Guitar Players and not Guitar Practicers.

Now that you can play songs, I want you to schedule at least 1 or 2 days per week where you pick up your guitar, put on a record, and just play.

The Playing Sessions can be as long or short as possible and they can even start spontaneously when you feel inspired.

The only catch is in a Play Session, you aren't working on anything.

Playing Sessions are all about effortless playing for your enjoyment and your escape.

These times are separate from your Fast Practice Sessions.

You'll still want to continue those every day if possible.

If you can't and you need to use one of those times to Play, then feel free to replace a Fast Practice Session with a Playing Session.

Hopefully, you can eventually set aside more time for more Playing Sessions, but never force it.

I want this entire experience to be as smooth and effortless for you as possible.

Now that you know what to do when things are going really well, let's talk about what to do when things go wrong.

DEALING WITH MISTAKES

Mistakes are such a fascinating topic to me.

Sometimes when you're playing and you're not thinking, you make a mistake.

Sometimes when you're playing and you ARE thinking, you make a mistake.

Sometimes you can play perfectly for the majority of a song and then a quick distraction (like a notification on your phone in the corner of your eye) can be enough to quickly derail your performance.

If you're going to play music effortlessly, you must know how to handle the mistakes you make.

Because you WILL make them…

…we all do!

Mistakes and the anticipation, prevention, or fear of making mistakes is the main cause of stress & tension for Guitar Players…especially Beginners.

This section should help to ease that tension.

LEARNING FROM YOUR MISTAKES

Let's start with a quick little exercise.

Put down the book for a second and go grab your guitar.

Seriously.

I'll wait.

cue elevator muzak

"…summer breeze, makes me feel…"

Ok do you have your guitar?

Good.

Now press all 4 fingers down in any random position in the middle of the fretboard without thinking about it and strum all the strings without thinking about sounding good.

CLUNK

Sounded pretty bad, huh?

I bet it did.

And that's great!

No, that wasn't a trick to make you sound bad for my personal amusement.

It was to prove an important point.

What happened after you made that mistake?

Did your guitar explode into microscopic pieces?

Did an angry mob storm your house in violent protest?

I doubt it.

Actually, I'm pretty sure there was ZERO consequence after you made that mistake.

And that's the point.

To show you that your mistakes aren't as big of a deal as you might make them out to be.

No one noticed or cared about your mistake.

And no one will notice or care when you make a mistake while you're practicing and when you're performing live.

This simple exercise of making a mistake on purpose could be the most liberating experience in your guitar playing journey so far…

…because it quickly proves that it's ok to make mistakes.

We have to go easy on ourselves and be ok with making mistakes.

I've played hundreds of concerts around the world, performing in front of almost one million people…

And I broadcast my guitar playing to thousands of people every week.

Thinking back, I'm not sure I've ever played a show without making any mistakes.

But the trick is, you can't really tell that I made any mistakes because I just got really good at covering them up.

And you will too.

If you're going to quickly play songs you love on guitar, you need to have a healthy relationship with your mistakes…

…because they are a natural part of the learning process.

The fear of making mistakes or the obsession with trying to eliminate all mistakes can create enough stress & tension to prevent you from ever playing songs you love…

…even simplified versions.

I see it all the time.

So the first step to dealing with your mistakes is to switch off your natural reaction of stopping immediately after making the mistake.

What you want to do instead is ALWAYS keep playing!

Always try to get back into the song ASAP.

Your natural tendency to stop playing after making a mistake (or at the very least, have a disappointed look on your face) is your inner-voice demanding you play everything perfectly.

And it can convince you that you don't know what you're doing or even discourage you from playing altogether.

No matter how long you've been playing guitar.

What you have to realize is that your mistakes don't really matter that much.

They're actually extremely minuscule in the grand scheme of things in your guitar journey.

So they aren't worth the frustration or emotional turmoil that they can cause some guitarists to experience.

Of course, when you're learning a song in a Fast Practice Session, you play two mistakes in a row (2MR) and those DO mean something.

They mean you will have to go back to something less difficult until you can play the Chunk 3xWMM.

But those mistakes are purely functional (no emotion necessary) and you need them to help steer your Fast Practice Sessions.

Now that you know that the mistakes you make aren't that big of a deal, let's talk about how to approach mistakes in a Playing Session.

THE TRAIN HAS LEFT THE STATION

When you start playing a song at home or on stage, you've effectively started a train that must keep going no matter what.

If you jump off the train (you make a mistake)…

…the train (the song) doesn't wait for you.

It just keeps going and going.

The same thing applies to playing along with records.

Once you hit Play, the song doesn't stop until it's over.

So you can't just start again from the beginning…

…or correct the part you just messed up and then continue playing.

The train is long gone by now!

What you want to do instead is listen to the record (or the other live musicians if you're in a band situation), figure out what section is being played, and then jump in with your guitar part to get back on track.

Kind of like those old TV shows where little girls are playing Double Dutch with the two skipping ropes.

Wait for the opening and then jump right back in.

It takes a little bit of time to approach your mistakes like this - where you are unaffected by the mistake itself and all you are thinking about is how to get back on track in order to make it to the end of the song…

...but I promise you'll get it.

I still react to my mistakes from time to time and they can still derail me if I'm not careful, so just know that nobody is perfect and it's just something you have to be aware of while you're playing.

THE TRANCE

What's interesting about making mistakes while playing for other people is you're often the ONLY one who knows that you made a mistake.

It isn't the Guitar-mageddon you originally thought it might be.

It's because when people listen to live music, they almost always get hypnotized by it.

Like they're in a trance.

And the bonus is if there's any singing involved (you or someone else), the audience's focus will automatically go to the singer, making your guitar part just a supporting element in the background.

How's that for taking the pressure off?

Here's one of my favourite stories about The Trance:

One of my students, Ben D., a 64-year-old Beginner Guitarist from San Marcos, Texas, recently crossed "performing live with Ronnie" (his older brother) off his Bucket List during a Memorial Day weekend festival.

Accomplishing this lifelong goal was a HUGE deal for Ben, and I wanted to do everything I could possibly do to help him have the performance of a lifetime.

One thing I discussed with Ben was that as long as he keeps playing and doesn't let mistakes hijack his performance, then he will make it through each song without breaking a sweat.

Ben: *"But won't the audience hear my mistakes? Won't that affect the performance?"*

Me: *"Nope. Not at all. The only thing that will affect your performance is if you stop playing and have a disappointed look on your face. Even then it would still be ok because you're playing with a band and chances are, the other musicians will keep going."*

That put Ben at ease.

So I asked him to arrange for the performance to be recorded, so he could have a video recording to commemorate the special occasion…

…and also, so I had something to watch and give him feedback on what went well and the areas he could improve on.

Ben did an amazing job!

He played "A Horse With No Name" by America and "The Joker" by Steve Miller Band.

Safe to say, I was very proud of Ben!

Bucket List goals are one of my favourite things to help my students achieve.

They are seriously life-changing and have the power to completely transform your belief system for what you can accomplish.

Ben was really happy with his performance and even happier to cross a lifelong goal off his Bucket List, but he told me he made a mistake during "A Horse With No Name" that almost derailed him.

When I watched the performance video, I didn't notice any major mistakes.

I mean, I saw that there was a little chord switch that was fudged during the Verse...

But Ben was performing with a band, so his error was completely covered up by the band and you couldn't even hear it.

If I couldn't hear it and I was looking for it, then the audience DEFINITELY couldn't hear it.

Plus, even if I could hear it, I wouldn't care because he kept playing.

The Train is moving...

The Trance continues...

To really drive the point home to Ben, we watched the video together and I pointed out the lady at the front of the audience, just to the left of the singer, who had a little too much Budweiser in her system during Ben's performance.

Don't get me wrong, she was having a great time.

In fact, she was pretty damn rowdy...

...riding an imaginary horse for half the song!

Do you think she noticed Ben's chord flub in "A Horse With No Name"?

Do you think she would care even if she did?

No way!

She was busy dancing with her friend, singing the lyrics, and having a great time.

And that's what you can expect from anyone listening to you play guitar.

Not that every audience member will be buzzing on Bud and doing the horse dance, but they will be talking to each other, grooving to the music, and just enjoying themselves.

The last thing they are doing is meticulously putting each note you're playing under a microscope and judging you on each one.

Maybe at a Joe Satriani concert. ;)

But even then, the crowd is often forgiving because you're the one on stage and they're not.

So if it isn't a big deal to make mistakes in a live performance situation in public...

...then why would it be any different in the privacy of your practice space?

It isn't.

LEARNING FROM MY MISTAKES

Ok, one more quick story for you...

This was my all-time BIGGEST failure live and it was ugly...

…at least in my mind it was.

Rewind to November 17th, 2012 at the legendary El Mocambo in Toronto, Canada where my band The Envy was playing a prep concert for our big headlining show.

We tried some new songs that night and also tried some new stage props.

You don't tour with KISS as the supporting act for 34 shows without having a different perspective on concert production.

We had to up the ante.

So being our ambitious selves, we thought it would be a good idea to have little TVs all over the stage that were all playing the same video footage synced up to different parts of the song.

It was actually REALLY cool!

So when we played one of our new songs called "Bones" - a song where my guitar part didn't come in until the 1:40 mark - I was supposed to hold a small TV in front of my face while my singer Shaun's face was on the screen singing his parts.

After the second Chorus, I was supposed to put the TV down, grab my pick, and enter with my lead guitar part.

A part that was in the middle of the fretboard and totally exposed when all the other instruments stopped playing.

And I had to do it all in what was pretty much pitch black.

Easy, right? ;)

All I remember was putting the TV down, grabbing my pick, and looking down to see that my fingers were one fret too high as I completely botched the entire lick.

But it's ok…it sounded even worse than it looked.

Yikes!

Playing a lick one fret higher is the same as saying "Basically every note I'm playing right now is going to sound like $#!†".

It was brutal.

However, since I'm a professional, I just kept playing as if nothing happened.

Gotta keep the train going, right?

I'd be lying if I said I didn't feel the sting from the mistake while we played through the rest of the song, since it was the worst performance mistake I've ever made.

But I just tried to shrug it off and have a good time.

Even though I made it through the rest of the show that night unscathed…

That mistake would stick with me for years.

I would always bring up the "Bones Blooper" when a student talked about their mistakes being a big deal.

It was my go-to example of things going wrong live.

But here's the funny thing…

Not only did nobody mention the mistake to me the night of the performance…

…one of my students recently found a video of the performance on YouTube and posted it in one of my Facebook groups for all the members of my online coaching program to see.

Just great!

My worst mistake ever available online for everyone to enjoy.

And that's when I had to come face to face with the infamous "Bones Blooper" once again.

Anyone bring popcorn?

So I loaded up the video, feeling a little bit tense in anticipation of the guitar part I was only ONE fret away from playing perfectly…

Where I accidentally turned a catchy guitar melody into the most obscure Jazz lick anyone's ever heard. ;)

And then the weirdest thing happened.

Believe it or not, I actually didn't catch my mistake on first listen!

I was in the same "audience trance" I described earlier and even though it was my song, my performance, and I knew it was coming…

…it flew right past me.

When I realized what happened, I snapped out of the trance and went back to the specific section of the video with the epic fail.

Let's hear this thing.

After putting the mistake under the microscope, I noticed two surprising things:

1) The blunder wasn't nearly as bad as I thought it was that night and it DEFINITELY wasn't as bad as how I described it as the legend of the Bones Blooper grew.

2) It almost sounded intentional, like a Grungy lick I played to connect the two sections together.

Not that I really liked the lick I played, but it definitely sounded like I meant to play it the way I did.

And that's probably what the audience thought as well.

If they were even thinking about it at all.

Which they probably weren't.

That's another secret of playing guitar.

If you play with intention…

…as if everything you play is supposed to be played like that.

And you couple that with good Mistake Recovery where you get back on track with the song almost immediately after making the mistake…

…then no one will even know that a mistake happened.

And when you can accomplish that, nothing short of a power failure can stop you from playing.

If you want to hear the Bones Blooper by the way, then I will include a clip on the PRACTICE LESS, PLAY MORE! Book Resources Page.

QUICK MISTAKE RECOVERY EXERCISE

Now let's get practical.

I want to show you a great way to practice your ability to recover from your mistakes.

The sooner you can recover, the better, so your goal is to always get back on track faster and faster.

All you need is your guitar and the record of a song you know how to play.

The exercise is to simply start playback from a random spot of the song, hit play, and then try to play along with whatever the guitar part needs to be at that point.

Maybe it's the second chord of the Chord Progression...

Maybe it's an Upstroke halfway through the Strumming Pattern in Verse 2.

Just hit Play at a random spot and jump into the track ASAP with your guitar.

No need to rush because that will probably lead to a moment of panic and could lead to a mistake when you enter.

At first, you want to take a second to think about where you are in the song when you hit play and then get the right part ready to jump in.

And then when you get the hang of the skill, it can be more instantaneous and you can jump in faster.

This is a really effective little exercise because most guitarists only know how to play a song from the beginning.

But that won't help you at all in a real-life playing situation.

When you think of where mistakes typically occur, it's often somewhere in the middle of the song or at random spots in the middle of a bar of music.

So if you play the record in a random spot and come back in with your guitar part ASAP, you mimic where an actual mistake would occur and give yourself the ability to develop your mistake recovery speed.

Have fun with this one and make it like a game where you try to jump into the track faster and faster!

Now let's talk about another element that will make your Playing Sessions successful, so you can play more songs in each session.

HOW TO KEEP YOUR SONG LIST ORGANIZED

In the beginning stages of practicing less and playing more…

You want to focus as much on getting wins under your belt, the practice habit programmed, and a few songs played.

It isn't as big of a deal for you to be super organized at the beginning.

However, once you're able to play about 3-5 songs, it's time to get organized.

So here's how I recommend doing it…

Create a new folder on your computer.

Inside that folder, create three new folders:

- MY SONGS (for MP3s to play along with)…
- MY TABS (for any TABS, chord diagrams, and lyric sheets you download)…

AND

- MY VIDEOS (for any progress videos you record).

You can get more specific than this, but three folders is a good start.

I personally prefer to have all the files on Dropbox (a FREE virtual hard drive that you can use to store files online).

The reason I prefer it is because I can access my songs, TABs, and progress videos from anywhere and on any device.

I just log into the site (**dropbox.com**) or my Dropbox app and it's all there.

No matter what type of hard drive you choose, just make sure to stay as organized as possible.

As I mentioned earlier, it may not be an issue now, but when you have a huge playlist of songs you can play and a ton of TABs and MP3s, it will be incredibly important for you to keep everything organized.

Save the MP3s and TABs you download to their corresponding folders.

If you have a physical songbook that you're using to learn a song, don't be afraid to mark it up with any notes or to indicate problem areas in the book itself.

You can also scan or take a picture of the page with notes to put in your TABS folder.

After you record a progress video, write the date, the song title, and something specific about what you're working on in the filename, so you can easily keep track of your collection.

Here's an example of a good filename:

"June 18th 2018 - Free Fallin' - Chorus Strumming Pattern.mp4"

This way, you can sort the files alphabetically and you'll be able to easily track your progress.

Also, if three months from now you need to remember how a certain part was supposed to be played on the guitar, you'll have an easier time searching for it.

You can set aside some time in every Pre-Practice Session or at a separate time once per week to watch a few progress videos from the previous week.

The shorter the videos, the more likely you'll watch and get the most value from them.

These simple organizational strategies will make sure you are making the fastest progress possible because they keep your mind clear of having to keep track of everything.

The more organized you are, the less time you'll waste finding the files you need.

And that ultimately means more time for playing!

STAYING ON TOP OF YOUR EQUIPMENT

The last thing I want to discuss in this chapter is equipment.

No, I'm not going to tell you about all the coolest gear you can buy.

You can reach out to me or connect with me on social media to chat about that.

What I DO want to talk about here is how to stay on top of your equipment so you can continue to make steady progress and prevent your guitar from biting you in the @$$.

It's a VERY real thing and not enough people are talking about it.

Your guitar equipment might be holding you back!

You might think your fingers are too small or too big…

Or you might not be able to play guitar because you never came from a musical family…

Or you might even think you can't play because your 6th grade music teacher told you that you don't have a musical bone in your body.

I've heard all the excuses…

And I've definitely made some myself! ;)

What you might not know is that a big part of whether or not you can play the songs you love relies on how easy or difficult your guitar is to play.

It sounds obvious, but it's a detail that's VERY easy to forget.

Just like I did back in late 2009…

I remember coming home after a 3-month national tour where I played to about 2,000-3,000 people every night.

It was a great tour, and I felt like I played really well at every show.

When the tour was over, I had about a week off where all I wanted to do was eat chips and binge-watch the TV show Dexter.

It was also just after Christmas, so I was staying up at my Dad's place for a few days.

Even though I had no plans to play guitar, I thought I would bring my favourite Strat anyway…

…just in case I felt inspired.

After a few days of lazy laptop lounging, I thought I would play some guitar.

So I grabbed the guitar from the basement and took it out of the case.

I tuned up and started playing.

I tried to play one of my favourite Muse riffs called "Hysteria", but it felt like my fingers were made of rubber and the strings made of concrete.

I just couldn't play anything and lacked total control.

And this went on for about 20 minutes before I gave up.

"What the???"

"It's only been 3 days since my last show…how come I'm making so many mistakes???"

I stayed there trying to muscle through it for another hour, and after an extremely frustrating string of more mistakes on parts I could normally play in my sleep…

…my confidence was shot!

I questioned everything about my ability to play guitar.

As if everything I've worked for was completely gone.

What a drama queen, right?

I totally understand how this sounds like a ridiculous thought for someone who had been playing for over 10 years at that point.

But it was VERY real for me at the time.

Our mind can really mess with us if we let it.

Especially when fuelled by a few bags of Doritos and countless episodes about a Miami-based blood spatter expert.

I should mention my Dad's house was always really dry, and it was the middle of winter, so it was particularly freezing that year.

And what I eventually realized before I sold my Strat to the first buyer online was that maybe, just maybe, it wasn't me.

Maybe it was the Strat.

I was travelling across Canada during the Fall & Winter months and the guitars were in the back of the tour bus every night where it was pretty damn cold…

…not the best conditions for metal strings and wooden guitars, which love to expand and contract.

I just didn't notice the gradual change in the setup of my guitar because I was so caught up in the tour and life on the road.

After a few days of not playing, the changes became clear.

So when I went to check the distance of the strings from the fretboard (the action), it was SO much higher than I remember when I set up my guitar before the tour.

It was like one of those old guitars you find at your Uncle's place that hasn't been touched in over 40 years…

…feeling almost impossible to press down the strings and play a clear note!

Like a recipe for Carpal Tunnel Syndrome.

Once I realized that my guitar was an absolute mess, I took a few minutes to set it up - lowering the action and replacing the strings - before trying again.

And as you probably would expect, once the guitar was fully set up properly, everything felt and sounded great again.

Phew!

If I wasn't careful, I could have spiraled into an extremely dark place where I would have doubted my ability to play for weeks…

…and lost the inspiration to pick up the guitar.

- Making excuses…

- Skipping practice sessions...

AND

- Basically, getting worse & worse to the point where I just didn't feel like playing anymore.

I hear about this kind of stuff all the time with Beginners & Struggling guitarists who are having trouble playing anything that sounds like music or have been trying to play for a while and are stuck in a rut.

Have you ever felt like that?

You might think that there's something wrong with YOU when sometimes it is actually something as simple as your equipment that's holding you back.

This is especially true if your guitar has never been set up, if your strings are too heavy, or if your guitar is an entry level guitar.

It seems ridiculous, but some low-cost Beginner Guitars are almost impossible to play.

The strings are far away from the fretboard, the frets are sharp, and you might hear an annoying buzz every time you strum.

No fun.

No wonder a lot of Beginners quit playing.

Even I have a hard time playing some Beginner Guitars...

...and I've been playing guitar for over 20 years!

I recently experienced this issue first hand...

A TRIP TO THE MUSIC STORE

Back in August 2018, I decided to buy my Mom an acoustic guitar for her 60th birthday (she just started learning to play).

My budget was about $300 for her gift and I had to play about 10 guitars before getting to one that felt comfortable to play, sounded good with no buzzing, and looked good.

Even some of the same models that look exactly the same can feel completely different.

How crazy is that?

It has to do with the fact that guitars are mass-produced on an assembly line, so it's almost impossible to make each one play well out of the box.

Hence, why I never buy guitars online no matter how good the deal is.

You have to experience playing a guitar in person to know whether or not it works for you…

…or you might have a nasty surprise similar to mine when the guitar arrives at your door.

YOUR TRUE LEVEL OF PLAYING

If this chapter is making you start to question your equipment…

A great way to test your actual ability on the guitar is to head out to your local guitar shop for 30 minutes and test out about 5-10 guitars.

Since you're not there to buy a guitar, focus only on playing guitars in the higher price ranges as they are usually built better, use higher quality parts, and are set up to play well so they can sell faster.

(You might want to leave your wallet at home just in case you feel tempted to sign this month's paycheck to Leo Fender)

Now that you're able to play a riff or two, you can feel a little more comfortable trying out some guitars in the store.

Just play a little bit on each guitar and what you might notice is your playing ability is SO much better, and it feels almost effortless to play.

This is your TRUE level of playing by the way.

And it's possible your current equipment is holding you back from achieving that level of playing.

No. I'm not telling you to rush out and buy that vintage Martin acoustic you tried or the $40,000 Les Paul that Jimmy Page allegedly sneezed on.

However, if it IS in your budget, either upgrade your equipment to the best equipment you can afford (after trying it of course)…

…or get your current equipment set up in a way that helps you play at your best.

Either way, I want you to experience your true level of playing and understand how equipment can affect your ability to play up to your true potential.

GENERAL EQUIPMENT RULES & GUIDELINES

Since your equipment can actually prevent you from playing songs you love on your guitar...

I've included some simple rules & guidelines below that my students and I are using to play at our best.

You don't have to incorporate all of them at once (or any at all).

They are just guidelines...

- As mentioned earlier, always try as many guitars as you can when you're at the music store no matter what your budget is (they all feel different and it's important you choose the one that feels and sounds great to you...not just one that looks cool)

- Make sure you're using the lightest gauge strings possible and change them once every 90 days (ideally once per month) - I would start with 9's for electric guitar and 10's for acoustic guitar

- Get your guitar set up every 6-12 months (every 3 months if you can afford it) and ask them to set the strings as low as possible without buzzing - this will make the strings easier to press down

- Use light picks to strum acoustic songs, medium picks for single string picking (i.e. leads), and thick picks for precision playing - I recommend Dunlop 0.60mm nylon (light grey) for strumming acoustic, Dunlop 0.73mm tortex (yellow) for general acoustic and electric playing, and Dunlop Jazz III (small red picks) for precision and speed playing - NOT MAX-GRIP!

- Buy a multi-pack of the picks you use because the point will eventually wear out and it will affect your accuracy

- Try standing up and playing with a guitar strap at least once a week - I like to set my strap, so the middle of the guitar is lined up with my belt buckle (sorry, Gene)

- Use a guitar strap even when practicing/playing sitting down (raise it much higher than you would when standing) - your shoulders will support the guitar and take the stress off of your fingers which will lead to more speed and more control

When you can play at least 5-10 songs comfortably on your guitar, you can start messing with different setups & different equipment.

For now, I recommend you use the guidelines above and always stay on top of your equipment, so you don't have any obstacles in your way to playing at your full potential.

If all else fails, ask a friend who plays, your guitar teacher (if you have one), or an employee at the guitar shop to test out your guitar.

Ask them to be honest with you about if it feels easy or difficult to play (i.e. the size of the body and fretboard, how hard they need to press the strings, etc.) and if they think it's the right guitar for you.

They might forget what it's like to start out and struggle on guitar, so have them imagine just getting started and if they think they would be able to successfully learn to play on your guitar.

There's a perfect guitar for you...

One that makes everything you play feel effortless.

Maybe you've already found it.

Maybe it's waiting for you at your local guitar shop.

Hopefully now you know everything you need to know to make sure you are always playing songs you love at your true level of playing.

ACTION ITEMS TO INCREASE YOUR SONG PLAYLIST

1. Pick up your guitar and make a mistake on purpose.
2. Set up your hard drive and/or Dropbox account and create 3 folders using the guidelines I mentioned above.
3. Get your guitar set up with light strings and low action.

* * * *

MORE READING/LISTENING

Visit **PracticeLessPlayMore.com** for a secret bonus chapter plus a list of recommended resources and additional notes that expand on this topic.

Chapter 11:
The Snowball Effect

Before we part ways, I wanted to shed some light on what you can expect in the next few months now that you can play a growing list of songs.

Some of the points I'm about to mention in this chapter may seem obvious to you, but I feel it's important for me to include them just to make sure you know them and there is no stone left unturned.

LEARNING SONGS MEANS LEARNING MORE SONGS

Arguably one of the coolest aspects to learning to play songs on guitar (besides being able to actually play them) is that after you learn a few songs, you will start to notice patterns & reusable sequences contained in each, which will make the songs you learn in the future MUCH easier & quicker to learn.

And this makes sense.

When you really think of it, music doesn't contain THAT many components.

For one, there are only 12 notes to choose from, which means there are only a certain amount of note & chord combinations that can exist.

When we look at popular genres like Rock, Pop, and Classic Rock, the list of possible combinations gets even smaller.

So when you learned the G, C, and D chord that was originally used to play "Time Of Your Life" by Green Day, you come to realize that that same G, C, and D, can also be used in "Sweet Home Alabama" by Lynyrd Skynyrd...

...just in a different order.

How cool is it that you can learn a chord or technique once and then use that chord or technique in multiple songs you tackle in the future?

I think it's amazing!

It's the same as investing where each investment compounds and creates a greater return each time.

In other words, the more songs you play, the more songs you're able to play...almost automatically.

That goes for chords, Strumming Patterns, legato techniques like hammer-ons, pull-offs, slides, pentatonic patterns, and the list goes on.

Also, some bands base their entire careers on having songs that are pretty much identical to one another in chords & structure (no offense AC/DC), meaning you can learn one song and you pretty much know them all.

Pretty cool right?

Here's what Angus Young had to say about that:

"I'm sick and tired of people saying that we put out 11 albums that sound exactly the same. In fact, we've put out 12 albums that sound exactly the same."

Classic!

THE POWER OF CONTRAST: THE SEQUEL

Even though I mentioned The Power Of Contrast in Chapter 9, I want to include it again here as a reminder for you to use it.

The reason for this is because I know that once you have a few songs under your belt and you develop more confidence about being a Guitar Player, you will be pretty much hooked on playing guitar.

And it's at this point that you can start to experiment with new techniques that are really going to accelerate your progress.

The Power Of Contrast is one of those techniques…

…as long as you go into it with the right mindset.

If you don't have any songs under your belt and you learn a song that is way too difficult for you to play *(and you don't know beforehand that it's too difficult)*, you will likely experience the Four Horseman of the Guitar-pocalypse:

- Frustration…
- Confusion…
- Overwhelm…

AND ultimately…

- A dusty guitar

It's hard to recover from that because it can completely kill your momentum.

However, when you flip the concept on its head and you go into the song knowing that its way too advanced for you to play…

…and you know that learning the song is just being used as a tool to make everything else you play on guitar that much easier in comparison…

…then you have one of the best Power Tools on guitar that I know of.

I can attribute most of my development on the guitar so far to The Power Of Contrast.

I've always been extremely ambitious, so it makes sense that when I was first learning to play, I'd constantly tackle more advanced material before I was ready for it…

- Joe Satriani
- Dream Theater

AND

- Genesis' entire Prog-Rock catalog

The list goes on…

Even though I've been self-taught for 22 years, I still understood at the time how trying to learn the advanced material *(even a small fraction of it)*, would mean that the more basic material I played would feel like a vacation and I could learn it that much faster.

Now I want YOU to experience the same thing my students and I do with the following guidelines to prevent any major momentum issues:

- experiment with The Power Of Contrast only after you have a few songs under your belt…
- only learn a little snippet of advanced material…

AND

- devote 1-2 days max to this experiment.

If you enjoy the experience and you can remain calm, cool, and collected throughout the entire process, then use this technique once a month.

If you hate the experience and get frustrated at all, stop and don't experiment with The Power Of Contrast until you can play more songs on the guitar.

Regardless, I want you to eventually incorporate a little bit of The Power Of Contrast in your guitar playing.

Challenge yourself to play songs in different styles and with techniques that you don't yet know how to play.

And you'll ultimately become a better guitarist because of it.

REVISITING OLD SONGS

One last note on learning songs.

If you're anything like my students, you'll often find yourself getting obsessed with a song and focusing on it almost exclusively for a couple of weeks straight.

After about two weeks, you might stop working on it because...

- You hit an obstacle that you don't know how to overcome...
- You feel completely satisfied with playing a simplified version of the song...

OR

- Life got in the way and you have to put the song on the back burner for now.

Going along with the theme of this chapter where success breeds more success...

One of the amazing things that will happen after you build up your Song Playlist to about a dozen songs is that when you revisit old songs after an extended period of time (i.e. a few months or even a year)...

...you'll often find that a lot of the parts that were challenging to play before are now easy to play.

And if they aren't easy enough to play right away, then they might only need one or two Fast Practice Sessions to iron it out.

So don't worry if you start learning a song, get stuck, and you have to put it away for a little while.

SIDE NOTE: Let me know if you are stuck at ANY time or if you are currently experiencing an obstacle you just can't get past on your own. You can message me at **support@rockstarmind.com** to let me know about the situation and we can discuss your options to break through.

If you DO put a song on the back burner, just leave it there and find inspiration elsewhere.

It's important not to dwell on old songs if they aren't inspiring you anymore.

Know that when you do revisit this song in a few months or a year, it will be SO much easier to play because you'll be leveraging the skills & techniques you learned in other songs while this one was on the back burner.

Pretty cool, right?

With this approach, your Song Playlist could all of a sudden go from 13 songs to 30 songs overnight.

And that's exciting!

CONCLUSION TO PART 3

The Snowball Effect is a real force that affects your song list, your guitar technique, and your confidence.

And once your confidence grows, there's really no stopping you!

Believe it or not, for me, it isn't about the amount of songs that you can play on your guitar.

Even if they're up to speed with the record.

Sure, that's an impressive feat and I'm really happy for you...

However, what I care about the most is that you are playing guitar, believing in yourself, and being able to confidently say out loud "I'm a Guitar Player!"

Feeling like the sky is the limit for you on the guitar...

...and most of all, having fun!

And that's what PRACTICE LESS, PLAY MORE! is all about.

ACTION ITEMS TO INCREASE YOUR SONG PLAYLIST

1. Spot 3 similarities between a song you know how to play and a song you want to learn to play.
2. Devote 1-2 days to an advanced song for The Power Of Contrast.
3. Mark a reminder in your calendar for 90 days from now to revisit the song you're currently playing in order to see if it's any easier to play.

---

* * * *

MORE READING/LISTENING

Visit **PracticeLessPlayMore.com** for a secret bonus chapter plus a list of recommended resources and additional notes that expand on this topic.

Conclusion & Next Steps...

It's Time to Play More Songs!

You did it! You completed the book!

I hope you learned a lot, and you enjoyed your PRACTICE LESS, PLAY MORE! experience.

I know any new system can seem a little bit overwhelming at first.

A very simple way to make it as easy as possible...

...to make it a game you're guaranteed to win:

Go back through the book, take the simple Action Steps included at the end of each chapter, and you'll eventually build a Song Playlist you can feel great about.

I've created the PRACTICE LESS, PLAY MORE! system to make it simple and easy for you to get results, as long as you **just do the work.**

You won't have to wonder again what your next step is because it's all laid out for you in the book.

My goal in writing this book was to free up your mind as much as possible while you have your guitar in your hands, because the last thing your mind should be doing is guessing what to practice next.

Just practice a little bit each day with your M.E.D.s, without worrying about if it's a waste of time or whether or not you are practicing enough "stuff".

You don't have to wonder if this system will work for you.

I know this system works.

My students know this system works.

In fact, it has worked for hundreds of my guitar students around the world.

If at any point, you are feeling stuck, you find something in the book that doesn't make sense to you, or you just need help…

…then you can ask me anything you want by emailing me at **support@rockstarmind.com**

And I will do everything I can to help you succeed.

And if you would like more structure & guidance than a book can offer…

…and you want me to help you use the PRACTICE LESS, PLAY MORE! system to play your favourite songs on guitar…

Then I highly recommend you check out my **Play From Day 1 - RAPID RESULTS Guitar Experience.**

Play From Day 1 includes step-by-step guitar training that brings the concepts of this book to life and shows you how to develop your Rhythm & Lead Guitar technique using the "create a game you're guaranteed to win" approach I laid out in this book.

I will work with you personally the entire time to give you feedback on your guitar playing, answer your questions, and simplify the songs you want to learn so you can play them from day 1.

Please visit the link below to add yourself to the waiting list and I will reach out to you as soon as spots open up and we can get started.

PlayFromDay1.com/waitlist

Whether you become a member of Play From Day 1 or you simply use the techniques in the book to improve your guitar playing on your own...

Thank you for taking the time to hang out, learn my strategies, and read my stories.

I definitely had a blast and I hope you enjoyed reading the book as much as I enjoyed writing it.

I can't wait to hear about your results as you Practice Less, and PLAY More!

Rock on and talk soon,

Steve (aka VØID)

STAY IN TOUCH

If you want to find out more about the ideas I've shared in this book, head over to **PracticeLessPlayMore.com**.

You'll find a special Bonus Chapter there for you to download— one that details the same approach I take to get even faster results on guitar with the help of software & apps.

If you have any questions, comments, or WINS you'd like to share with me, please email me at **support@rockstarmind.com**

You can also connect with me on:

Facebook: facebook.com/steveakavoid
YouTube: youtube.com/RockstarMindTV
Instagram: @rockstarmind

Come hang out with me at my weekly #PajamaJAM on Facebook where I learn popular riffs and solos up to speed in 30 minutes or less LIVE on camera.

I explain everything I'm thinking as I practice, so you will be able to see a lot of the concepts from this book in action.

Visit my Facebook page and follow me to receive notifications on the next #PajamaJAM.

I look forward to hearing from you!

ACKNOWLEDGEMENTS

I may have written this book in only 5 days, but it took 22 years of incredible experiences and a lot of really great people in my life to make it happen and I have many people who I'd like to thank for making it all possible.

First, I want to thank my wife, Desirée, for always believing in me, being patient with me, and always being my cheerleader while I was figuring out my shit. I love you so much, muhluv.

My daughter, Milana Soleil, who spent the first year of her life making my heart melt and making me laugh hysterically every single day. You were the inspiration for finally writing this book, Tee Tee, and my drive to finish it all in less than a week.

My Rockstar Mind customers & subscribers, for investing your time, money, and energy into my learning strategies. You are the lifeblood of Rockstar Mind and I appreciate you very much.

The members of my Play From Day 1 & my Band coaching programs, you are my sounding board, my Idea Incubator, and my support system. Your trust in me means the world to me and many of the ideas contained in this book were created because of conversations we had during our lessons and Rockstar Repair sessions.

My long-time students and friends, Johnny Warda & Chas Demain, for reading the first draft of this book and working with me to make sure it clearly communicates my voice and my message. I couldn't have done this without you guys!

Gene Simmons, for giving me the opportunity to perform in front of thousands of screaming fans each night. I'm extremely grateful for all the insights you shared with me as well as the lifetime of epic stories & memories I now have from working with you.

My coach, James Schramko, and my friend, James Eager, for recording the podcast that activated me and lit the fire under my ass to finally start writing this book. That was a magical day that pointed me back to my North Star and I'll never forget it.

My mentor, Ryan Levesque, for teaching me to imitate before I innovate and that I don't have to get it perfect, I just have to get it going. As a recovering Perfectionist, I really needed that.

Sandeep Likhar, for helping me lay out this book so it could look great in multiple formats and clearly communicate my ideas with aspiring guitarists around the world.

My AMAZING launch team, for taking time out of your busy schedule and really putting your all into the launch of this book, so that more guitar players around the world can play beautiful music. We did it! You have no idea how much it means to me that you were part of this experience with me.

My business partner, Ryan McKenzie, for helping me organize the next chapter of my company Rockstar Mind as well as keeping me sane and laughing until it hurt during my entire first year of fatherhood.

My songwriting partner, bandmate, and best friend, Shaun Frank, for willingly going on the adventure of a lifetime with me and enduring the endless ups & downs of the music industry together.

Dave Candito, for giving me the first Classical guitar I learned on, Steve Saroli, for selling me my first electric for 50 bucks, and my brother from another mother, Evio Martellacci, for letting me play your red Strat every time I came over (it played SO much better than my shitty electric). I wouldn't even play guitar if it wasn't for you guys.

And finally, my parents, Tony and Rita Mastroianni, and my sister, Jenni, for always encouraging me while I pursued my dream of touring the world performing my own songs. Sorry I was so loud.

I love you all.

ABOUT THE AUTHOR

Steve Mastroianni (aka VØID)

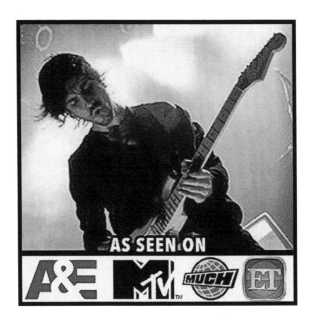

Hailing from Toronto, Canada, I have been a self-taught Guitar Player for over 20 years, a professional touring musician for 10, and a guitar coach for over 15.

I've had the rare opportunity to tour the world opening for bands such as KISS, Hinder, and Finger Eleven as well as get hired to perform live with my childhood heroes Our Lady Peace in front of 60,000 screaming fans...

In 2013, after putting my budding music career & dreams of Rockstardom on hold to become my father's primary caregiver, I wrote this on the back of my guitar:

"I BELIEVE I CAN INSPIRE + HEAL WITH MY <u>GUITAR</u>."

Within five years, I have helped over 20,000 Beginner & Struggling Guitarists around the world quickly play their favourite songs on guitar, while using proceeds to create new programs for Cancer patients and their caregivers in honour of my late father Tony Mastroianni.

100% of the proceeds from this book are being used for the same purpose through my fundraising initiative VØID Cancer.

I have a deep-seated passion for helping people reach their true potential on guitar and become the best version of themselves.

So what's in it for you?

Put simply, I have the unique perspective of being both a guitar coach and a touring guitarist, so I get to share with you all the guitar techniques that you'll actually use in the REAL WORLD without any fluff...

As well as the ability to transfer my knowledge to you in a simple way that you can easily understand.

My specialty is helping you create new habits & routines in your life and making the complex world of guitar simple, so you can make steady progress on your guitar even in the most challenging of circumstances.

I truly care about your success and I highly value the personal connection shared between student & coach because I strongly believe it plays a major role in you making the fastest progress possible.

Anyone who knows me will agree.

So on that note, if you have a few minutes to spare and you want to know more about me, please head over to **VoidCancer.com** where you'll find a short video with a more detailed story about me and my mission.

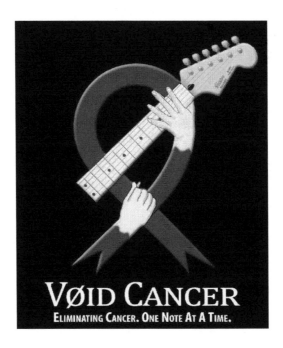

It's only about 5 minutes and I urge everyone I teach to watch it.

And if you would like to share YOUR story with me, please send me a message at **support@rockstarmind.com**.

I read every single message myself and will do my best to reply back to you ASAP.

Made in the USA
Lexington, KY
26 February 2019